My Guy

A Gay Man's Guide to a
Lasting Relationship

MARTIN KANTOR, M.D.

SOURCEBOOKS CASABLANCA™
AN IMPRINT OF SOURCEBOOKS, INC.®
NAPERVILLE, ILLINOIS

Published by Sourcebooks, Inc.
P.O. Box 4410, Naperville, Illinois 60567-4410
(630) 961-3900
FAX: (630) 961-2168

Library of Congress Cataloging-in-Publication Data

Kantor, Martin.
My guy: a gay man's guide to a lasting relationship / by Martin Kantor.
    p. cm.
Includes index.
ISBN 1-57071-967-5 (alk. paper)
  1. Gay male couples—United States. 2. Mate selection—United States. 3. Interpersonal relations—United States. 4. Gay men—United States—Attitudes. 5. Gay men—United States—Psychology. I. Title.

HQ76.3.U5 K33 2002
646.7'8'086642—dc21

2001032271

Printed and bound in the United States of America
BG   10   9   8   7   6   5   4   3

This book is dedicated to Michael.

Acknowledgments

Three people have been of great assistance in getting this book together. Virginia E. McCullough has worked with me over the years to help me create and edit my books, Barbara Levine has acted as my agent, and Deb Werksman, my editor for this book, has contributed her considerable editorial knowledge, creative ability, and patience with a restless and sometimes intrusive author to keep things going throughout the process of writing and shaping this volume. I also want to thank Michael for being a combination of sympathetic ear, antidote to nerves, cure for reactive depression, and Exhibit A, who reminds me daily of the benefits and joys of a lasting relationship, and of what it was like without him.

Table of Contents

Introduction

Finding—and keeping—a partner is the single most important challenge in gay life today. Years of counseling gay men who are looking for, but not connecting with, Mr. Right have taught me that too many gay men are alone when they don't want to be, even though there are plenty of lovers out there; relationships are, theoretically at least, not that difficult to find; and opportunities for love and marriage exist in the gay world for just about everybody.

It seems to me that too many gay men are spending their entire lives either physically distant from each other in isolated, rural, small towns or physically close but emotionally detached from one another, living anonymously in big cities, together, but just barely, in noisy bars, the baths, or pornographic movie houses.

Some gay men are comfortable with their arrangements. Other gay men would like to connect but aren't very good at it. They find making the transition between the solo and the domestic life tough, and full of obstacles to success. They begin to wonder if they should even bother trying. They tell their friends they want a long-term relationship, only to hear in reply pessimistic predictions and a repeat of the latest myths circulating in the community about gay relationships, things like "a gay golden anniversary takes place when a marriage is fifty days old." Discouraged, they turn to books written for gay men on how to meet other gay men, only to find little more than superficial advice, too light—or lightweight—in approach. For one reason, the books shy away from dealing with unhelpful mind-sets and the emotional baggage they create. For another, they tell gay men how to find Mr. Right, but not how to be one, so that the Mr. Rights of this world will find them. They forget to tell them that settling down with the man of their dreams also means being in his.

Three Core Messages

This book outlines my approach to the problems gay men have connecting meaningfully with one another so that they can create lasting love relationships. My approach emphasizes the importance of taking charge of your life and taking responsibility for what happens to you, individual mastery through self-awareness, and the rewards of hard work and devotion to the cause of creating a great relationship for yourself and your lover.

In the realm of taking charge of your life and taking responsibility for what happens to you, I ask you to recognize that it's mostly you who determines the outcome of your search. You are more in control of your relationships than you think, and blaming bad luck or your stars when things go wrong makes better balms than plans. Do you make a habit of blaming the world for all of your problems? Instead, put yourself in the equation of your life and recognize that it's not only where you live, homophobia, the attitudes of other gay men, or gay life itself that holds you back, it's that person you see in the mirror. In this book, you'll learn how to look in the mirror to ask what you can do to improve your image, not to discover what is wrong with the glass.

I seriously believe that if your life seems dull and empty, it isn't because you don't have what it takes, it is because you haven't taken what it has. More than likely, you have all the pieces you need to play the mating game. For you, as for most gay men, life could be wonderful, if only you would let it be. Since you are reaping what you sow, you can change your life simply by changing the way you plant your field.

In the realm of individual mastery through self-awareness, I ask you to understand your fears and anxieties about connecting. I give you insights that can help you make fewer dating mistakes as you eliminate internal obstacles to being happy, successful, and in enjoyment of your life and your relationships. *What do I want out of life?* is sometimes not the most pressing question for gay men to ask themselves. Sometimes that question is, *I already know what I want out of life, so what are my personal resistances to actually getting it?*

Personal resistances to connecting occur on an emotional level and, therefore, can affect your strategy. That's why working both on your emotions and your strategy is the best way to release the power you have inside of you to make romance happen. In the realm of emotional resistances, deep problems like social anxiety can seriously compromise your motives and short-circuit your motivation directly. In the realm of strategy, social anxiety often creates practical problems indirectly. For example, you might look for love in all the wrong places, because instead of going where you might meet Mr. Right, you only go to the places where you feel the most comfortable. That doesn't mean that solutions to every relationship problem are complex and difficult. While some strategic problems require complex solutions—meaning that you might need to work through internal obstacles and resolve a wide range of difficulties that interfere with getting a lover—sometimes it's enough just to learn to relax and discover what a simple wink and a hello can do.

In the realm of the rewards of hard work and devotion to the cause, I ask you to be serious about love and looking for a lover and to accept that it isn't all fun in every moment. As with pearls, when love doesn't grow on its own it has to be cultivated. It's an old wives' tale that relationships happen when you least expect them to. What looks like an unexpected windfall so often is just the successful outcome of good planning. Don't expect to round the corner and walk right into love. Give more than lip service to wanting to improve your relationships. Effort and follow-through are required, and distractions—such as giving first priority to wearing stylish clothes, having a well-decorated apartment, or coming out in a politically correct way—interfere. These only lead to lazy and unfocused dating, and that leaves this most important part of your life entirely subject to chance.

This is a serious book on connecting, as befits the importance of its subject. It is written specifically for gay men who may be turned off by the cynically humorous approach taken in other books about gay relationships, approaches that seem to exemplify rather than solve the problem.

There is very little guesswork going on here. My book is based on clinical experience—formal studies of the lives of gay patients I have treated professionally, as well as informal studies of gay men I have known personally as friends and acquaintances. In all cases, names and identifying information have been changed in order to protect the anonymity of the people in the story. In addition, many of my insights and observations come from candid comments that gay men who are alone and still complaining about it made in bars and restaurants, unaware that anyone was listening in a professional capacity.

When it comes to advice about who will make a satisfactory lover, mine included, everyone has some to give, but you should think twice about taking all of it. When it comes to giving advice about psychological matters, too many people are experts. For example, some talk show hosts are making it up as they go along. They have never actually seen a patient or client and generally haven't had the insight that comes from sticking around to see if there are bad complications from all the good advice they give. So be sure to filter any advice you get through your own better judgment and ignore anything you aren't certain works for you. My outcome studies have shown me that many gay men have profited from my advice, and that you can too. I cannot promise that all my suggestions will work for you, but I can assure you that they are doable and effective, with most of the kinks ironed out and the major bugs removed. There's more here than just the kind of advice you have already heard a thousand times before or thought of yourself—familiar old saws like developing awareness, honesty, and commitment. Mine is a broad-based, comprehensive approach that goes beyond one-dimensional explanations and narrow solutions. Instead, I offer you suggestions on how to improve not only your relating techniques but also your frame of mind. It's no good going out armed with advice unless you like yourself well enough to feel sufficiently empowered to use it. I also offer you many suggestions so that you can try out a number of different approaches. When it comes to successful relating, trial and error is often the best way to make it work.

I also tailor my suggestions to you as an individual. People are different, and what works for others might not work for you. I help you pick and choose among my menu of suggestions so that you can come up with an individualized plan that fits *your* special gifts, qualities, and preferences. Good solutions should be to your problems, not to someone else's. For example, if you are a bold gay man willing to take risks, then for you it's "nothing ventured, nothing gained," but if you are a shy, more reluctant type, then being safe is better than being sorry, and you should go slowly to avoid paralyzing failure and devastating rejection. Gay men who fear close relationships may need to work on their problems with commitment, while gay men who like merger relationships (or are what I call "positively codependent"—two hearts beat as one and serious separations are unpleasant or dangerous) can forget about problems with commitment and work on accepting their dependency and finding someone similarly inclined.

This is a focused book, too. It's about finding a man you can keep. And it's a book about mating, not a sex manual. Indeed, in some significant ways it is the opposite of a sex manual. One of my major premises is that too many gay men who are looking for a committed relationship put sex first and relationships second when it should be just the other way around. They say they are looking for a husband, but they act like they are looking for a harem and completely fail to recognize that different attitudes and methods apply in each case. Then they get lots of sex but no partner, and blame that on the gay life rather than on their specific lifestyle choices. The personal ads provide far too many examples of how looking for sex and looking for relationships don't necessarily mix, and how an interest in exchanging body fluids can be incompatible with an interest in exchanging wedding rings.

I don't overlook sex, however. After all, sex is very important to gay men. Why else would our honeymoons regularly take place before our weddings? I just limit my focus to those sexual problems that occur in the context of relationships. I point out that sexual problems don't start or stop in the bedroom. They tend to take over your personality to create trouble on, as well as off, your feet. In a vicious cycle, sexual and personality problems reinforce each other, so that a problem with impotence in bed spreads to become the limp handshake that, right from the start, says, "We aren't going to get it on," making it less likely that you will ever get him to bed and even have to worry about whether you will be impotent.

I believe that when taken together, my suggestions add up to a basic approach to connecting with other men. It is one that will stand you in good stead not just today, but until you find the man of your dreams. This basic approach is a great gift because you can apply it, and keep applying it, throughout your life until success is yours. A professor of mine once said, when criticized for not knowing a certain obscure fact, "I may not know that, but I know where to go to find the answer." The gay man aware of his limitations and how to go about compensating for or correcting them is the gay man prepared to prosper under the most wide-ranging and difficult circumstances.

My approach to finding a lover carries you through from desire to achievement. First, I outline nine steps for you to take in searching for love, including ways to overcome obstacles to seeking a lover. Then, I address some special situations and concerns, like ways for gay men who are getting older to improve their chances of finding a partner, how to overcome sexual problems, and when to seek further assistance. Finally, I help you develop an action plan, one that will turn thinking into doing so that you can actually meet that man of your dreams, Mr. Wonderful.

The Nine Steps

The first step to establishing a committed relationship is to learn about relating and loving. I emphasize the different styles of relating that you can pick and choose from, and then I make my case for the benefits of seeking out a close, committed, monogamous relationship. Next, I try to open your eyes to fictions about relating and love—myths you might have heard and subscribed to, but are detrimental to seeking a committed relationship. Then, I describe some Mr. Wrongs to avoid (so you won't fall in love with someone who doesn't meet your needs, or love you in return) and some characteristics of Mr. Rights. In my chapter on tactics, I give you some concrete suggestions on where you might go to find Mr. Right, not only the bars, but other places like Chinese restaurants at peak take-out times.

It also helps to know what to do when you get there so that you don't screw things up. That's part of the process of becoming Mr. Right so that Mr. Right can want you. You should look great and be great, developing all those endearing personal characteristics that make you Prince Charming. I also have some suggestions on how you can worm your way into his heart using win-win techniques to encourage someone previously disinterested in you to take notice and want to get to know you. From here, the dating process may go smoothly, but many gay men need to overcome any one of a number of obstacles to an effective search for a relationship, such as inertia, fear of loneliness, fear of rejection, or a lack of focus.

Effective connecting requires more than adequate motivation, sound logic, and relative freedom from crippling myths, cognitive errors, distancing tendencies, and poor self-esteem. You need good positive personal qualities. Before you can find Mr. Right, you have to be Mr. Right. When you ask, "What are the qualities I seek in Mr. Right?" also ask, "What will make me Mr. Right for him?" When you ask, "What do I see in him?" also ask, "What does he see in me?" I suggest a number of good personal qualities to have and show you how they make for good luck, which is more attitudinal than you might think, depending as it does on sincerity, warmth, empathy, and other attributes that give you a good reputation in the mini-world within which you are looking and that are indispensable to getting the "referrals" you need to find what you are looking for.

Gay men often become love-averse when they let their anxiety and fear take over and put a gap between themselves and those with whom they want to be connecting. Promiscuity is often a central part of this process. I define promiscuity and show you how, as a form of distancing, it can negatively affect your relationships. In my opinion, promiscuity is the best illustration of how great sex can be the single biggest enemy of great relationships.

Tactics are sensible, often obvious ways to do things that you might nevertheless have overlooked. No tactic is inherently good or bad, right or wrong. A tactic is good if it creates new opportunities without using people in a hurtful or manipulative way. A tactic is bad if it doesn't work out or harms others.

Developing good tactics helps you find a permanent relationship just by making a few simple procedural changes. It involves a new approach to making contact in a more organized, productive, and effective way.

Gay men with tactical problems manifest some emotional difficulties too, but these are secondary to their isolation. Within this group, depression may be a reaction to loneliness, or anxiety may be a kind of existential yearning for unattained or lost companionship. Tactical problems tend to respond to education and training. In a virtuous cycle, those who improve their tactics and skills have fewer emotional problems; those who have fewer emotional problems improve their tactics and skills.

If you are a gay man with good tactics, you know that when you're looking for a relationship you are on stage, and that if you muff your lines, you lose your audience. You know where to go and what to do when you get there. You practice the right moves and know how and when to make them. You play the odds to increase your chances, often incrementally. You improve your luck of the draw by knowing what games to play and when to take your gains and cut your losses. You develop effective approaches to men that help you get their attention and whet their appetite. You use all the opportunities that are available to you. You try to connect with strangers face-to-face and use the personals—writing and responding to personal ads effectively, yet honestly. You know a few good opening lines, and a few effective bar-cruising gambits, too. It's not that difficult to take on these good tactics, and this book will show you how.

A major tactic I'll be covering is networking, which many gay men use effectively. They build an interlocking meshwork of good friends, "sisters," and short-term sexual relationships, people who know people who know people to introduce you to and who are on the lookout for you. Building a network requires patience. Like building a foundation, it can seem to take forever. You may not see the point of networking until, after months of digging and cementing, the first outlines of your brand-new house suddenly shoot up above the ground. Thus, persistence is another important aspect of connecting. Developing relationships takes time and cannot be forced. Though you may wish it weren't the case, relationships rarely happen overnight. Mostly, you have to keep on keeping on.

After you have gotten started, you might discover that it is not enough to develop the skills and strategies you need for finding a partner. You may also need to drop some of the emotional baggage you've been lugging around. By unburdening yourself now, you can fly.

Improving your sex life is important, and I discuss this in the context of, not as an alternative to, your relationships. For those of us who believe, as I do, that familiar expressions reveal primal emotions and deep motivations, the expression "screwing up" tells us in two little words how too much sex can leave you with too few relationships.

Finally, it is important to know when and where to seek help if you need more help than I can give you. Psychotherapists can amplify on some of the material I present and answer some of the questions I raise in this book, moving you even further from here to there.

I conclude by developing an action plan for life. There are two ways to change your life for the better. One good way is to make plans first and then put them into effect. Another good way is to go before you are ready and set. Most people say, "Think first, act next," but I show you some of the advantages of doing it just the other way around. And, actually, backing and filling—doing both simultaneously—is often the most productive method of them all.

I base my advice to you in part on what worked for me. I went through all the stages, from being promiscuous to going straight through psychoanalysis (alchemy?). I've had a wide variety of relationships, from a committed relationship in name only through a sadomasochistic relationship where my lover drank himself to death to my present relationship with Michael, which is a variety of a merger relationship. It's strictly monogamous, and we haven't spent a night apart since we began in earnest. We have both become nice and quiet and ordinary. We use the same toothbrush and have basic sex which gets better by the week. I toned myself down and beveled my sharp edges. I put adolescent experimentation behind me just in time for menopause and embarked on a new experiment in living, full of the pleasure, warmth, and stability that I think is only possible when you have a great partner for life. For me, the freedom from aggravation is one of the most wonderful things about being in a committed relationship.

I would like to share one last word about the tone I adopt and the terminology I use. At times I do go for the easy laugh, but only to make a serious point. If I am occasionally flippant, it is because I feel that sarcasm sharpens darts and guides them to the bull's-eye. However, I avoid gratuitous humor because I have discovered, from overhearing the really serious camping that passes for seduction scenes in some circles—both gay and straight—that for the gay man looking for a lover and thinking that heavy camping is the way to find one, it is too often "laugh and you laugh alone." I do some preaching too, but that is only because I have the fantasy (obviously impossible) of officiating at your upcoming wedding. I haven't found the perfect label for two men in a committed relationship or the perfect name to give that committed relationship itself. Should I speak of lovers, significant others, boyfriends, partners, serious singles, spousal equivalents, or husbands? And are two men together in a partnership, a committed relationship, married, or what? Should I try to blur the distinction between gay and straight relationships by using the term "marriage" for both, or should I emphasize the differences by speaking not of married couples but of "partners" and "committed relationships"? I have decided to retain the term "marriage" (and related terms such as "husband" and "divorce") as generic terms that approximate but imprecisely define the emotional and legal nature of the goings-on in committed gay relationships. I use a term like "marriage" the way I use the term "sister": like the term "gay" itself, to simultaneously convey a meaning that is tongue-in-cheek and deadly serious, one that is untranslatable for those looking for a straight equivalent. I ask people who feel that my usage of these terms is too striking and too literal to envision quotation marks around them each time they occur. Now they will seem less inexact, more justified, and free of invidious comparisons to the same concepts in a heterosexual context.

I know from my personal experience and from helping patients move from here to there that togetherness is more than an abstract criterion for happiness and a theoretical good. It provides a lifetime of peace and joy, and I hope that you know that peace and joy will be yours. I send you off on your daily tasks with my well-wishes and the hope that you will write to or email me to tell me all about your progress (martycando@aol.com), the new man in your life, and your fabulous wedding with the meaningful ice sculpture of two drakes blissfully entwined and melting into one.

1

Step One: Choose Relationships and Love

Some gay men who are by themselves like their life just the way it is. Other gay men who are by themselves spend their entire life just hoping and waiting for their luck to change. They dream about getting together with someone and putting the whole pickup scene behind them. They are getting older. Everything and everyone begins to look the same. They feel unfulfilled. They are drinking too much or taking too many drugs. They fear that they will get a disease and it will kill them. They used to dream of Mr. Humpy Number. Now instead they dream of Mr. Wonderful. They have decided: it's time to start thinking about having a committed relationship. Their focus has shifted from Eros to heroes.

Your first step should be making exactly this shift. Decide for yourself that you are ready to be relationship material, and you'll be surprised at how your life shifts too.

Various Styles of Relationships

Various styles of relationships and various types of arrangements are possible for you. The main ones include exogamy and endogamy (defined later), and the different sexual preferences. It's easier to know what you want, and to get it, if you know what the possibilities are.

Different or Alike: "Opposites Attract" or "Birds of a Feather"

Relationships can be classified according to how different or alike the two men involved in them are. In the different, or *exogamous*, style of relationship, contrasts are a big part of the attraction. In the alike, or *endogamous,* style of relationship, it is the similarities that attract.

You've seen both: the gay man with his polar opposite, and the gay man whose partner is his mirror reflection. Exogamous men avoid other men who are similar in superficial matters like age, appearance, wealth, or sexual prowess, and sometimes in deep matters like personality traits and important attitudes about sex and fidelity. Examples of men who appear to be deliberately seeking their opposites are the Asian who must pick a non-Asiatic, the older man who always chooses someone younger, and the elegant man who only likes rough men, with no other situation acceptable. Naturally, exogamy or endogamy also arise out of social pressures—to move up in the world or to stay with your own kind. As I go on to explain, social pressures help bring exogamous or endogamous relationships down, too.

What at first glance looks purely preferential can in fact be partly determined by an individual's past history. For example, exogamy often starts with a need to dissociate yourself from, defy, and get back at your parents. Sam was a disenfranchised man whose rebelliousness took the form of picking the men of whom his parents would most likely disapprove. He just couldn't wait to see his parents' faces when it was "eek week"—or, "Mother, look at what I dragged in." Because he was castle born, Sam preferred men who had just arisen from the moat.

At the other extreme from exogamy lurks endogamy, where you pick someone as similar as possible to what you are, or—and sometimes this is the same thing—as close as possible to what would be acceptable to your parents. One goal is to fulfill your dreams of falling in love with yourself. Yours is the relationship that tempts others to say that you don't even have to look in the mirror to shave. Another goal is to submit to parental authority and marry a nice boy, someone from your own class, someone who won't embarrass your father and mother.

Compliant Roger never developed a normal, healthy rebelliousness. Instead, throughout his life he let his parents guide his every move. Partly as a result, he now favors lovers he believes will please and impress his parents. For him, life reached its apex when he lived in San Francisco and his parents visited him from New York. He was thrilled to be able to show them he lived with two beautiful men: Arthur, who was his roommate, and Ron, who was his lover—and on some days the other way around. Of course, it was silly for Roger to even think he was impressing his parents with this arrangement.

Each style of relationship has its own advantages and disadvantages. Successful relationships can exist between men who are very different, quite alike, or closely but not exactly matched. But exogamy and endogamy can increase the chances that a relationship will end in failure. That is because men who make extreme choices often set the stage for later problems, not because the men are different or alike, but because they are, or become, incompatible.

When people are too different, they can compliment each other but they can also have very little in common. Some people cannot ultimately live with someone too unlike themselves. They like themselves too much just the way they are for that. Consider the problems likely to occur among the following pairs: sloppy/neat; faithful/promiscuous; rude/kind. You can see the difficulties associated with picking someone out of a conviction that opposites attract.

When people are too much alike, they may have much in common, but they may also spend the rest of their lives in "sibling" rivalry. In addition, gay men who pick lovers to please and impress their parents or some other authority figure soon get restless and want someone for themselves, that is, someone entirely of their own choosing.

In addition, exogamists and endogamists greatly narrow their fields of choice. When age differences and racial differences are either a source of attraction or repulsion, you become a specialist, or even a fetishist, and statistically that makes it even harder to find someone because your selectivity reduces the number of available possibilities.

Social pressures that create endogamous or exogamous relationships can also bring them down. If you are coupled with someone different from you, expect to hear dishy remarks—your lover is too young, too old, not successful enough, too successful for you, not of the same race, and so on. If you are part of an endogamous couple, expect to be accused of marrying yourself. Criticisms like these are especially difficult to handle because exogamy and endogamy in the first place arise, at least in part, out of a need to be loved. Exogamy is often the equivalent of a prolonged temper tantrum about not being loved completely by those closest to you. Endogamy is often a sustained attempt to get the love you want, in the form of approval from mother herself, or from a mother substitute.

Sexual Preferences

Sexual preferences of the partners offer another way to classify relationships. Bisexuals are often important in the lives of gay men, just as gay men are often important in the lives of bisexuals. Some men marry a woman and have kids, and have sex with men on the side, just as some men commit to a man and have a woman and kids on the side. Some men who are homosexual, not bisexual, marry a lesbian for show, often for professional reasons, to have what looks to the casual observer like a heterosexual family.

Role Models

Another way to classify relationships is according to the role models adopted by the individuals involved. Sometimes there is a man-woman division of labor—what some refer to as the Latin American model. There is the Greek model where an older man becomes mentor—and more—to a younger one. The third model involves a relationship between two men who do not differentiate along such clear preset lines, but instead share roles and responsibilities. Often, but not always, they are about the same age, and more or less from the same social background. They often look about the same and have essentially the same hopes and dreams. However, endogamy (where like is attracted to like) is not an important issue in such relationships, because the initial differences between the men are significant, and if they look insignificant it is because the two men have grown to become, and sometimes even to look, alike.

Level and Styles of Emotional Commitment

Relationships can also be classified according to how close or distant the two members of a couple are. There are different styles of commitment, varying according to intensity and exclusivity. Some gay men live together and are faithful to one another; others are close but faithful in varying degrees. Two men can still be a couple if they live on different shores, or have individual relationships outside of the primary relationship.

Commitment, being an emotional matter, can be, and often is, detached from sex. This is appropriate or not, depending on how the individuals involved and those who evaluate them look at it. Here again, there are many different possibilities. Some gay men feel that sex is sex and emotional commitment is emotional commitment and you can have one without the other. Some gay men feel that this is impossible, because you are less committed if you are out all night looking for someone else or feeling left out because your lover is off looking for or staying with someone else.

I personally prefer to view sex and commitment as two sides of the same coin. If you need to look away from home, then there is probably a strain in the relationship, and that might be something that needs to be fixed, not acted on. Besides, one of the biggest reasons for divorce is meeting someone new, something that is much more likely to happen if you are meeting many people in the course of maintaining a relationship.

Some men have merger relationships. Here, two men become, in effect, twinned. They do everything together. They go to work separately, but apart from that one never lets the other out of his sight, and they are absolutely faithful sexually to each other. Some mergers are asexual. They are mainly for companionship, and, aside from occasional diddling, not much goes on sexually, though much may have happened earlier in the relationship. Many psychologists frown on merger relationships. They don't distinguish hostile mergers, where people get close out of spite, and affectionate mergers, where people get close out of love. They think of all mergers as primitive, or condemn them as codependent, their way of saying that too much closeness just isn't healthy. Such statements discourage people from having what is, in my opinion, a fine relationship that is additionally a great way of coping with life, very pleasurable and rewarding, and altruistic and loving. Merger relationships are more common than we think, because most of us don't know many merger people who often exclude others from their lives. Also, many men in merger relationships live outside of the cities where much of the research on gay sexuality takes place. Even the experts think that mergers are mainly confined to lesbians, but in my experience that is simply not true. Indeed, I have a modified merger relationship myself, and I happen to think it's great.

Sexual Arrangements

Issues of fidelity and commitment are extremely important in gay relationships. Your thoughts about what you want are important in determining your choice of partner. Here are the possibilities.

Monogamy

There is monogamy short of merger. Monogamy can be orthodox or reformed. Orthodox and reformed monogamous types differ in a way that reflects deeply divided attitudes both about sex and the quality of relationships: specifically, how close to get versus what limits to maintain.

Orthodox monogamists are as strict about their minds wandering as they are about their bodies straying. When they fall in love, it is completely. For example, Roland, one of my patients, expected Carlos, his lover, to avoid pornography entirely because Roland felt that when Carlos looked at pornography, it was just another way to embarrass, humiliate, and reject him. When Carlos looked at pornography, Roland felt inadequate, abandoned, depressed, and suicidal because he felt overshadowed, ignored, and even disgusted. Roland thought "he likes someone else better than he likes me," and that started him brooding about the time that his mother responded to his father's frequenting go-go bars by feeling inferior and rejected, to the point that she got a breast implementation to compete with the go-go dancers.

Roland, like most orthodox monogamists, didn't believe in even talking about his past sexual escapades to Carlos, and he certainly didn't share his private sexual fantasies with him. He even cleared the house of all pictures of and correspondence with old lovers. An old lover from forty years ago wanted to revive a friendship with him, but though Roland really liked the guy he said no. He even refused to have an email relationship with him, because, as he saw it, that could only sabotage his relationship with Carlos.

Roland was also willing to tell white lies for his relationship. Like any other married man, he had extramarital sexual fantasies, but he suppressed them. He thought them, but he did not say them. He kept them, but he kept them to himself. If he slipped in his thoughts, he kept it quiet—a good idea since it just isn't worth hurting a partner for the elusive goal of complete honesty. He rarely slipped in his words and, consistent with the definition of orthodox monogamy, he never slipped in his actions.

Orthodoxy insinuates itself into the personality, carrying over to affect how a gay man behaves with his lover. Men who are orthodox monogamists are often involved, intense, interested, focused, faithful, sensitive, and empathic men, from start to finish. Clearly, such men make very good husbands. Their chief downside is that they can be a bit overbearing, which, in my opinion, is not a bad trade-off. You have to decide if you feel the way Roland felt and want what he wanted. Then, if you do, you have to avoid self-questioning and stop letting the society you live in discourage you from going after it. Look for someone who doesn't force you into an arrangement like, "No outside sex at home, but outside sex is OK when I am away at a convention." Don't accept such an arrangement because you think that accepting it is better than having him leave you.

In contrast to orthodox monogamists, reformed monogamists relate in body but not in soul, doing everything but "it," and with everyone else but "him." Victor looked but didn't touch. He went to the baths but "only" as a spectator. Jim, his lover, didn't like it, but he said nothing for the good of the relationship, which otherwise was OK. Victor wanted to look. Jim decided to look away. I wouldn't want to be Jim myself, but this kind of relationship works for some.

Reformed monogamy carries over into one's personal life, too. As a reformed monogamist, Richard, a personal friend, came across to Jim as a reluctant partner who only agreed to monogamy because he felt Jim would have left him if he cheated. Richard and Jim would still be married today if not for Richard's death, but the relationship was always strained because Richard was unpredictable, unreliable, dishonest, and interested enough in others to always be somewhat unavailable to Jim. Many gay men have a relationship like this, and it seems to last. Whether it works is another matter entirely, and there is much disagreement in the gay community about this. Don't agree to this kind of relationship, if it's not for you, just to be one of the boys and a part of the freedom movement that might look as if it's everywhere these days. Tell yourself, and everyone else too, that successful relationships are built on saying no to certain things, and that a good place to start saying no to lust is with your man's wanderlust.

Bigamy

Bigamists take the next step (up? down?) from reformed monogamy and have two full-time lovers. A bigamist typically promises his secondary lover to leave his present husband and marry him, while having no real intention of doing so. He does this because he wants to have it both ways. So he establishes Byzantine schedules for servicing two partners, juggling them like inanimate objects, things with no feelings.

Bigamy also spills over into the personality. Most bigamists are self-centered people who expect their primary partner to suffer without complaining and their secondary partner to stand in line while the bigamist finishes whatever he is presently doing. Typically, the bigamist will break important promises to both partners. These men act in an imperious fashion, one that appeals mainly to gay men who prefer being subjects rather than being objects of affection. Bigamy, rarely containing the growing desire for sexual variety, tends to change over into polygamy or promiscuity.

Polygamy

Polygamists are "sultans" who have a closed or semi-closed harem of steady tricks. They have many relationships, but the number does not approach infinity the same way it does with promiscuity, and the whole structure tends to remain, at least in the short-term, a closed system. Each of the many men tends to serve a particular, special purpose for the "sultan." The sultan usually has one primary lover—the one he keeps for commitment, the one with whom he had that commitment ceremony, you know, the event that will always be remembered for that slightly used and soiled bridal gown. He even fools himself into thinking of himself as "basically faithful," using rationalizations like, "sex is a physical act without emotional implications." The sultan keeps secondary lovers, too. He splits people into various parts, gives each a special role to play, and uses each for a different, often selfish gratification. One is to surrender to him, one to surrender to, one to beat, another to be beaten by, another to bring his youth back vicariously, another to tease ("Well I thought I could come over tonight, but Hugh came home unexpectedly, and so we will have to make it tomorrow instead."), another for warmth and comfort, another for hot sex, and the list goes on. This setup is one of the few wholes that amount to decidedly less than the sum of its parts.

Polygamy also affects the character, and not in stellar ways either. An imperious, controlling, selfish attitude tends to develop and make polygamous men undesirable to anyone not looking for a casting director to decide what role they should play in life. Polygamists also get a bad reputation within the gay community for being "loose," paradoxically even with gay men who are themselves promiscuous, or themselves advocate promiscuity. The whole bar scene knows the polygamist, and usually isn't too discreet about passing the information on, so that his reputation precedes him to a new contact, possibly endangering any serious design he might have on him.

Promiscuity

The significance of promiscuity varies according to whether it occurs as a developmental phase; has become a distancing behavior; is an accepted feature of a relationship, that is, it is a relationship "style"; or creates tensions in a committed relationship.

In the realm of a *developmental phase,* probably the days are gone when gay men go directly from virgin to married (maybe those days never existed). Probably, most gay men start out by being promiscuous. In terms of psychological development, promiscuity is OK in adolescence, however prolonged the adolescence is, where it is part of coming out and growing up. Many gay men continue to show a preference for promiscuity well into their adult lives. These men do not want one man but a menagerie. They cite the advantages of promiscuity, and there are some good things to be said for it. As they say, "new" sex is exciting, "old" sex can be boring. Promiscuity also discharges tensions. It can substitute for another, more troublesome emotional problem like anxiety or depression. It can also provide an infinite variety of thrills not available to those men who are monogamous: the thrill of the pursuit, the catch, and the triumph over high (personal, sexual, and medical) odds. Don't forget the bragging rights that come with promiscuity, too, as your "sisters," wide-eyed with open mouths, hang on the every hairpin turn your tales take, foreswearing dishing you for being the whore of "babble on," at least until after you have left the room.

Promiscuity can be a search for monogamy as well. Sometimes, the intent is to get close to many men in order to find a compatible partner. And it's true: meaningful relationships can grow out of sex as much as sex can grow out of meaningful relationships. There is also some truth to the saying that the more men you try, the more likely you are to succeed in finding a lover, making promiscuity a little like playing the lottery—the more tickets you buy the greater your chances of winning.

Distancing promiscuity interferes with finding a long-term relationship when a gay man goes beyond having different experiences before settling down, and goes for quantity at the expense of quality. In such cases, a gay man uses promiscuity not as a way to get close, but as a way to hold people off. Such promiscuity has only disadvantages. This sort of promiscuous man makes any potential lover feel unwanted. He comes across as reluctant to form a committed relationship and sometimes he coerces a new lover into accepting an arrangement he doesn't want and might resent.

Distancing promiscuity signals, and is the product of, ingrained, self-sustaining compulsions to push people away. Typically, this kind of man doesn't want to be promiscuous, but he doesn't make the choice. Instead, the choice to be promiscuous is made for him. He doesn't necessarily want to live the promiscuous way, nor does he fully accept the promiscuous lifestyle. He might even complain about his own behavior, but he doesn't seem able to stop it. He is promiscuous almost in spite of what he consciously intends. The basic problem is often a fear of commitment, but hostility to others and self-destructive trends exist too.

Gay men who have gotten used to being this way run the risk that when they find a lover to whom they want to commit, they will not be able to stop being promiscuous. If you are one of these men, sometimes you can do a U-turn, but it can be difficult to break a pattern of promiscuity because the underlying reasons for it persist and because, as with anything else, practice usually makes perfect. Promiscuity as a distancing behavior is discussed further in chapter 9.

In another form, promiscuity is an *accepted feature of an otherwise committed relationship*. These relationships often last too, but whether they are as rewarding as monogamous relationships is the subject of much controversy within the gay community. What is certain is that not all committed relationships where one or both parties are promiscuous are exactly alike. You might do the extracurricular sex on your own, or you might do it with your partner in the form of threesomes or orgies.

Most of us think that all gay men do that. But that's because we tend to know the ones that do. They seem to be in the majority since they are the ones that invite us over. They may not be a majority, however, and from my personal experience there are more committed monogamous relationships out there than most people think.

Promiscuity can create *tensions in relationships* due to the sexual behavior, or for secondary reasons. For example, many promiscuous men are away from home a great deal. Like bigamists, they establish complex schedules to service more than one man at a time and expect all concerned to stand in line waiting their turn. They can be elusive and dishonest and make a lover angry over breaking important promises and being unavailable sexually as well as emotionally.

Falling in Love

You are in love! Yes, the desire to love is as much a factor in homosexuals as it is in heterosexuals. It often signals that adolescence is coming to an end and adulthood looms, or, as some would say, threatens. Every single gay man I have ever treated and known has at least expressed the desire to find a lover, fall in love, and settle down.

I've read a number of essays on how to distinguish mature love from adolescent love or puppy love, but I've concluded that it cannot be done. Crushes, hero worship, impulsiveness, and no sense of the need to be practical at all are just as characteristic of mature love as they are of adolescent love. In my opinion, the only real difference is that adolescents are more honest and direct about their feelings, while adults are more interested in putting a good face on them; adults in love are just as wacky as adolescents, only less willing to admit it. The feelings are nearly the same, but adults are often more motivated and better situated to deny the troublesome ones.

There are a number of myths about what love is, many of which are touted as the last word and litmus test for you to use to decide if you are truly in love with him and he is truly in love with you. Most of these are little more than overly rigid rules that disregard individual differences and the considerable complexities of loving feelings. They also define love in a circular fashion, as in, "Being in love is being willing to go to the ends of the earth for him, and a willingness to go to the ends of the earth for him is being in love." Following these rules, you can supposedly distinguish between love and lust (love starts with the head and goes down to the crotch, lust goes in precisely the other direction), true love and infatuation, love and dependency, love and projection ("he loves me" from "I love him and dream of his loving me"), and you can even decide if there is such a thing as love at first sight, and if you are experiencing it.

But the rules aren't very good. There is no real way to decide if you are in love. Love is a very personal thing. There are many kinds of love, each of which conceivably fills the bill. Love is a Rome you can get to by many roads, and once you have arrived you are pretty much in the same place no matter how you got there. In real life, love consists of many things, not just one. It consists of unequal parts of lust, idealization, desperation, and, perhaps particularly, hope, and is, in addition, an arrangement you like, want, and need. All these things together, or any combination of them, can be love. You can be in love if you mainly idealize him without knowing him well at all, if you are a lonely sinner and he is your St. Bernard, or for almost any reason at all. Certainly, there is no way to use specific conclusions about "Is this love?" as the basis for making important decisions about whether to pursue a relationship or not, and whether to make it an affair or try to turn it into a close, committed relationship. There are many reasons to commit to each other. Love, affecting your judgment as it does, may not even be the best reason to get married. Practical considerations are often as important as emotional responses.

There are no good rules to follow related to the process of falling in love either. There is no right timing for falling in love any more than there is a right tempo for all music. We often hear, "Don't be too quick to fall in love." We almost never hear, "When it comes to love, seize the moment." Those who condemn love at first sight as unreliable and insubstantial too often forget that love at first sight belongs to that class of first impressions that steer you right on multiple-choice exams. My experience with gay relationships tells me that some gay men have been together for years after falling in love at first sight and getting married soon afterwards—sometimes holding the ceremony and deciding to move in with each other during the first orgasm. In other cases, this is just a sign of impulsiveness and premature evaluation, the kind of thing that gives people cause to believe that everyone who falls in love at first sight and gets married falls out of love at second sight and gets a divorce.

My suggestion is that you stop obsessing and playing word and mind games, which can cause breakups, because you think your love isn't exactly kosher. Don't tie yourself in knots defining love according to one of its characteristics and then think you or he isn't in love simply because a specific criterion isn't met. Obsessing away about "Is this love and am I really in it?" can cause you to discard perfectly adequate men because they don't exactly fit into your definition of what you want in—or think you should feel about—a relationship.

The only ceremony to stand on is the one that takes place at your wedding. Go where your instincts take you, but make sure you don't burn any bridges behind you on the way (such as selling your apartment or giving up a good job to move across the country to be with someone you just met on the Internet). Then, if things don't work out, you can always retrace your steps and start over again. Especially if you are young, settle down first, then count your blessings next, and if the count comes up short, just leave while there is still time. Your heart will break either way, if you avoid him or if you break up. So it's better to love and lose—and you know the rest.

How Do You Define a Relationship That Works?

I define a working relationship according to the stability and the happiness of the individuals. There is no real correlation between stability, happiness, and style of relationship. Dick and Ralph have been together for forty years without any real sexual commitment, but the emotional commitment is intense, and they are very happy. Frank and Carl have been together for forty years too, and they are absolutely faithful to each other, but they do it out of guilt, misplaced altruism, and spite. They always seem unhappy, fight a lot, criticize each other brutally, say they are going to go to divorce court and find someone better, then never even make a move in that direction. What makes a relationship last, work, and be a happy one is very elusive. The desire to make it work is often enough to do the trick—if only because it motivates you to overlook a lot.

What Is So Great about Relationships Anyway?

A lot of gay men question the value of a committed relationship on the grounds that it means abdicating to one man (and to the whole establishment), retreating from your gay identity, and giving up your rights to mess around guilt-free. I look at committed relationships somewhat differently. I see them as purely gratifying and as having nothing but advantages for both parties. Here are some of them.

Some people admire the quietly married gay man more than the promiscuous single. Being admired, in turn, increases your self-esteem. You will have more money, too, since DINKS (gay men with double income and no kids) are often able to live better than SINKS (single income with no kids). You have a life outside of the gay ghetto and an improved social life, too, for now you have an "in" with the many men who limit their friends to men who are, or have been, happily married. Companionship, an ally in the daily struggles of life, and domestic bliss are waiting for you too. You can forget about those dumb hobbies and being surrounded by the things you love (inanimate department only), a life of camping with "sisters," and those terrible Saturday nights and Sunday mornings—in the dark all by yourself, awakening to yet another lonely hangover and the music stations playing the same Top 40 selections over and over again. You will feel better physically and emotionally too, because love heals. Panic to find someone is gone, replaced by quiet satisfaction with what you already have. Your married "sisters," whom you used to think had it all, envy you instead of the other way around. You won't get depressed about what is missing from your life—because nothing truly important is. Pessimism about the future, with odds growing bleaker by the day that things will ever improve in your life, is a thing of the past, and you no longer have to look to the promise of each fresh morning as your only compensation for the pain of each lost yesterday.

Your health improves because you are no longer so exhausted and depleted all the time. Nobody rejects you, at least in ways that really hurt. You improve your personality too. You become less selfish because you now consider someone else's feelings, give to another person, and renounce such superficialities of life as the trivial thrills of sex on demand. You finally go from an unstable adolescent (bitchy, rebellious, impulsive, angry, self-preoccupied) into a stable adult (kind, cooperative, rational, forgiving, concerned for others.) When the time comes, you will be able to give a good answer to the question some think you might be asked in heaven: "What did you do with your life?" Now you can proudly say, "I had a lover, I spent it with him, I made him happy, and it is enough."

A stable relationship liberates you to do other useful things, like creative work, either alone or with your lover, as you give up your constant cruising and the distractions that go with it, and draw your attention away from more meaningful activity. (See the list of distractions in chapter 9).

Sex gets better too. Ever wonder what it's like to have sex with only one man for twenty years? It improves and improves by the month. It gets to be a good habit. You can enjoy it without worrying about any consequences, and you get double the pleasure and double the fun from all the cumulative warmth and love. A monogamous relationship makes the heart grow fonder and practice with the same person makes perfect. Having sex with the same man over and over doesn't get boring. A basic behavioral principle is that with some things, the more you do them the more you want to do them.

Finally, you can also now look forward to a happy future. Freedom is great when you are young. However, behavior that works at eighteen no longer works at ninety-five, as your options diminish. Many gay men who wished for the freedom to do as they pleased when they were younger discover that when they are older they cannot find too many people to do it with.

In Step One, you have successfully climbed high enough to know what's out there (almost anything you want). Now you can gear your actions to finding exactly what you desire. You have learned that you first need to decide that you want a relationship and then give some thought to exactly the kind of relationship you want. That's important because it determines what you are looking for in a husband and even where you should go to find him. As you can easily imagine, a leather bar is not necessarily the right place for you to look for Mr. Loving.

You are now ready for Step Two, which is to do a reality check of the myths about the availability and viability of what you want and your chances of getting it. Without these myths bedeviling you, you are in a better position to aim for falling in love and having a committed, monogamous relationship. Love and relationships are the sustenance that will keep you from becoming lonely and depressed; they are also the catalysts that make sex better and better as time goes by, making bigamy, polygamy, promiscuity, and cheating less and less appealing and necessary. Sex is only one part of life. It certainly isn't more important than other people's feelings, including your own. I believe the sooner gay men stop denying this, the sooner they will be at peace with themselves and be able to get exactly what they want and deserve.

2

Step Two: Do a Reality Check

In this chapter, you will learn to develop an optimistic view about your chances of forming a long-term relationship by doing a reality check of the many negative myths and automatic, illogical, often totally silly, cynical thoughts in circulation about gay love. These beliefs could conceivably hold you back from important self-improvement and could prevent you from finding and keeping a lover. Getting these thoughts out of your mind, putting in some new and better ones, and thinking more positively is Step Two. Taking this step helps you search for love more effectively as you become more open to new possibilities in men; start being more hopeful about relationships; start seeking out the really wonderful men out there; appreciate men whom you previously overlooked; and strengthen your signals, beaming them in the right direction and correctly receiving and decoding the positive replies.

For example, I often hear gay men say, "Don't look there (the bars, straight restaurants, fill in the blank), that's just a waste of time." Charles, a patient of mine, bought it when his friends told him that the gym culture was for morons and that if you exercise at all it should be at home, not in the gym with all those gay men full of pretense and narcissism. He continued to think in this rut until one day I was able to convince him to try going to the local athletic club. When he went, he was surprised to discover that he liked it there. He found the Cybex method appealing, because he could build muscles without breaking a sweat. The same men who ignored him in the bar talked to him in the gym, partly because he had an attractive body, and partly because he acted healthier in a healthier setting. By going to the gym, Charles grew in a new and important way. He had learned a specific new tactic for meeting men and he had started doing what worked for and pleased him—not everyone else.

Some Helpful Truths

Here are some facts to counter some myths currently in circulation about the quality and nature of gay relationships.

Pessimism about Gay Relationships Is Not Warranted

The pessimistic view about the success rate of gay relationships can easily discourage you from looking for Mr. Wonderful. The pessimistic view interferes both with being motivated to search and with successful dating. More optimistic ways of looking at things can help you spot what you want and go for it without preconceived negative notions from the gay community, from envious "sisters," and from knuckle-rapping parents who can discourage you from finding a committed relationship, cause you to toss aside a perfectly good prospect before thoroughly checking him out, or impel you to walk out on a perfectly fine relationship already in progress. They can also convince you to agree to arrangements that go against your grain (as when you agree to accept a lover's cheating on you when you really want him to be faithful to you, or go along with someone who right from the start tries to convince you that monogamy is for sissies). They can infect you with cynicism and unhealthy skepticism to the point that you become its spokesman yourself, and infect others in turn.

Here are some examples of pessimistic modes of thought that gay men frequently employ. The first is that *rejection is devastating,* the thought behind the aphorism that a pessimist is an optimist who has just been rejected. Another is that *if something can go wrong it will.* A pessimist subscribes to Murphy's Law, which is just wrong-headed thinking based either on taking a limited sample or on having a limited perspective. Many things go right on a day-to-day basis. It is only the Murphys of this world who don't seem to notice this. They only remember the man who got away, just as they only remember the subway train that didn't come. Then they get depressed, stop doing the things they need to do to succeed, and retreat from the world, nursing their wounds and hurt feelings. They judge the behavior of all gay men based entirely on the misbehavior of a few. They believe their own negative prophesies, which then become self-fulfilling. They think in circles, as in, "I cannot meet anyone because I don't have what it takes," and "I don't have what it takes because I cannot meet anyone." If you are one of these men, vicious cycles and rut thinking can make you feel desperate and cause you to back off, panic, or say to yourself, "Why bother?" In a panic, you might stay up late at night cruising. When you are a wreck the next day, that can translate into a feeling of hopelessness. That leads you to become even more frantic to meet someone and cruise even more, which means you get less sleep than ever and are even more of a wreck afterwards. This makes you feel even more like a failure, so you act frantic; and so on.

A pessimist overreacts. He thinks that just because some gay marriages do not work out, all gay marriages are doomed (so why bother looking?). A pessimist condemns the bar scene entirely just because of some of its admittedly dreadful aspects—or never replies to personal ads because some of the ads are written by people who are more fabulists than fabulous. A pessimist thinks, "If he isn't all good then he is no good at all," or that lusting after someone now means that any relationship that develops cannot possibly last.

Being an Optimist Makes Sense

Be an optimist and never consider withdrawing completely from the scene just because there are problems associated with trying to meet Mr. Right, or because you see gay relationships that are imperfect. Never think that because most of the time you don't meet anyone in a bar, you can never meet someone in a bar. Don't think that just because some gay men cheat on their lovers that fidelity and monogamy are impossible in gay life. Realize that cheating isn't always a problem and breakups are not inevitable. A gay golden anniversary doesn't necessarily take place after fifty days, and people don't always have a seven-day itch—or if they do, they don't always scratch it.

Realize that if you think gay relationships don't work, it is only because the most married of men are the most private of people. The gay relationships that work just go on and on without calling attention to themselves, and so without your knowledge of them. I can assure you: the impression you get about gay life from the Gay Pride Parade is quite different from the impression you get about gay life from attending church or synagogue in a small town. If you travel in the "singles circle," you probably tend not to travel in circles of gay men involved in happy, long-term relationships. The ones you do run across are often cheating on their husbands. This is not a representative sample.

Not All Gay Relationships March to a Different Drummer

Being gay defines a group within which there are many subgroups. Gay relationships range in style all over the map, from the heterosexual model, where you have a house in the suburbs, a two-car garage, one or more children, and large outstanding debts on your credit cards, to the one where you and your lover grow older separately. Automatically buying into the idea that a picket fence isn't right for gay men makes it likely that you will compromise what you want and are willing to accept in a lover. If you want that picket fence, go for it, then get him that set of His and His towels for the bathroom the two of you just redid.

It's Not Possible to Predict the Future Based on the Past

Many gay men attempt to predict a gloomy future for themselves based on the bad things that happened to them in the past. They think, "Because the last man I was attracted to didn't like me, the next one won't either." Making predictions doesn't work in the stock market, and it doesn't work in relationships.

You Can't Tell in Advance Who Is Right for You

You don't know with any degree of certainty right from the start who is Mr. Right and who is Mr. Disaster. I know from my personal and professional experience that you just can't tell up front which relationships will work out and which relationships won't. So avoid making too many rules for yourself about who you should or want to become involved with. Following what you consider to be a basic rule like, "Type A men never get along with Type B," can lead you to reject a great prospect, and following a basic rule like, "Love at first sight is lust, and true love takes months or years to develop," can lead you to avoid someone simply because you find him attractive. Trial and error is usually the best way to find out if the two of you are compatible. That's because the catch-22 rule applies to all relationships, gay and straight. I know of no way to overcome it. You should know someone well before you get married, but you cannot know someone well until after you are married. So, don't hesitate to get involved and see where your feelings take you. If you fall in love at first sight, that's perfectly OK. With time as your ally, you can reevaluate him as you go along. I advise you to err on the side of following your positive rather than your negative feelings. Feel strongly but act wisely. Remember that it helps to take small steps when you do not know where you are going. Just do not burn any bridges or sign over the farm while you put your love to the test of time, which takes more than a night and less than an eon. And good luck.

You Are Good Enough for Mr. Right

Many gay men get a reputation for being immodest. They think if A = B, and B = C, therefore A = C, as in, "Judy Garland is not a virgin, I am not a virgin, therefore I am Judy Garland," and, "Models strut on a runway, I strut, therefore I am a model." Or they think, "If I love him, he loves me," as in, "Isn't he gorgeous, just my type? I am convinced of my chances, so I'll spend the rest of the night going after him and ignore everyone else."

Unfortunately, using the same kind of reasoning, gay men can also come to just the opposite conclusion and think of themselves as flawed. They begin to think, "Gay people reject people; he is gay, therefore he will reject me." Now they become completely unglued. Stop jumping to negative conclusions based on this sort of faulty thinking, and instead of thinking, "Flawed is my middle name," just change your middle name.

You Are Handsome Enough for Mr. Right

Many gay men put a premium on looks and feel inadequate because they aren't drop-dead gorgeous. In reality, you don't have to be really, really cute to find a man. It sometimes looks that way because you notice extremely good-looking men the most, and maybe others don't make such a big impression on you. You may have to be good-looking to get a man who is good-looking to fall in love with you at first sight and have a one night stand with you. And it does help to be good-looking if you want to have a "twin" relationship with someone else who is good-looking.

But real life is different. In the real world, I have known plenty of couples where one is more attractive than the other, or where neither is attractive at all. First, some good-looking men don't like other good-looking men because they don't like the competition. Second, what is good-looking to one person is not necessarily good-looking to another. Third, most gay men prefer having committed relationships based on qualities other than looks.

Be careful not to let a negative evaluation of your own looks hold you back; others see you differently than you do. Looks are subjective, and are highly influenced by positive personality characteristics, such as a degree of self-confidence that prompts others to be confident in you. Work with what you have. Make your own good looks with good grooming; keep your body up by going to the gym; keep your teeth clean and white; and, perhaps most important of all, develop a positive attitude that shines forth in nonverbal signals, such as an immediate welcoming response to an attempted seduction that makes him feel wanted and accepted.

In fact, it is very common for gorgeous gay men to have low self-esteem. Believe it or not, many gorgeous gay men think of themselves as ugly and believe,

"Anything is good enough for me." Thinking he believes himself too good for you and that he outclasses you, you stay away from him, and he stays away from you because he fears you will reject him and confirm his belief that he is undesirable. Just saying hello and looking interested can be enough to make you look as terrific in his eyes as he looks in yours.

Besides, there is a built-in biological need for humans to connect that is not much different from the one in animals, and like any other need, it leads to overlooking the facts. Before becoming unduly pessimistic about your prospects, remember that while some birds are prettier than others, I have never yet seen a bird without a husband. Nor have I ever met a gay cardinal who says he got involved with his mate strictly because he adored his red color.

Pushing Is Not Counterproductive

If you are in love with someone who doesn't love you very much—that is, if you are having a one-way affair, really stalking your quarry in hopes that he will change his mind—don't just let him go, forget about him, and move on. Plenty of relationships start off with one pushing and the other pulling away, and then work out. Often these roles can reverse, when the puller becomes the pusher. My caveat, however, is to give yourself a reasonable time period. If, at that point, you're not making progress, you might want to cut your losses and pursue another possibility. The biggest problem you will probably have is when that nice man you wanted more than life itself comes around five years later, but it is too late because you are already married.

The thought, "If love is meant to happen it will happen," only leads to stalling. Going slowly and being overly cautious has significant dangers of its own. While going fast with a cautious type can overwhelm or threaten him, going slowly and being overly cautious can not only be passionless, it can work against you in situations where mixed feelings about you exist, especially with men who are sensitive and dependent. If they think you are taking too long to respond, they are likely to feel insulted and rejected, lose interest in you, and find

someone else. Being coy and mysterious, claiming uncertainty, waiting and waiting until you ask for his hand in marriage, and not saying "yes" immediately
when he asks for yours, can increase the chances that he won't stick around even
if he is actually falling in love with you, but will instead go on to another person
just because you kept him waiting. As a result, you might suffer a serious,
irreplaceable loss.

Get out there and strike up a conversation, even though doing so makes you
a bit anxious. For starters, try doing little things, like just saying hello—or hello
back—to people. Instead of taking one day at a time, make the days dovetail into
one long continuous effort to meet Mr. Right. If you do take one day at a time,
you might forget what you are doing and where you are going and backtrack over
and over, wasting a lot of effort. Baby steps are great at the outset, but as soon as
you can, give up those baby steps and start to leap over tall buildings—and all the
other obstacles in your way—in a single bound.

A number of my patients with anxiety, social phobia, or avoidant personality
disorder problems—that made them shy or even forced them back into the
closet—have responded to pharmacotherapy. There are some medications that can
help you if you are very anxious. (This might be something to discuss with your
doctor.)

Here's a related idea to reality check, too—the idea that you should always be
extremely cautious before moving in with him. If you take a poll asking how long
you should know someone before you move in together, you will mostly hear
warnings to go slow. But are these warnings overcautious? They probably represent
a cynical view of gay relationships as being composed of people who jump into and
out of another's apartment as quickly as they jump into and out of another's bed.
Perhaps they signal the presence of a significant measure of snob appeal—after all,
redefining gay relationships along special, often magical lines, is very
sophisticated, isn't it? Possibly, too, someone has just found in your behavior yet
another reason for rapping your knuckles. I feel that when you move in doesn't
matter as much as if you can move out again, comfortably, if things don't work

out. Make sure that before you say, "I do," to a move that the move is for richer, not poorer, an expression of your health, not of your sickness. Then get moving.

Networking is a great idea for those of you personally averse to pushing. As a cornerstone technique for finding a lover, it is a fail-safe process that gives you a support system to fall back on and keeps you from rushing into situations that create more anxiety than you can tolerate. It is a good compromise between doing nothing and being bolder that you can handle comfortably. I discuss networking more in chapter 9.

Relationships Are Liberating, Not Confining
Relationships do not destroy individuality. They are its ultimate expression and, ultimately, your best chance at self-fulfillment. Try to put your needs for personal freedom on the back burner. Don't see potential lovers as moving in on you and crushing you. Being yourself includes yielding to the natural urge to merge.

Love Is Not Just for Sissies
The belief that expressing love is sissified is a very common one and it is one that usually comes from our culture. It is harmful because it can be a convenient excuse to maintain preexisting conflicts about positive feelings by not admitting them to yourself.

Playing Hard-to-Get Isn't So Smart
Review your opera librettos and remember what happened to classic teases like Bizet's Carmen. My advice to you is to display your affections freely, and affirm and reaffirm your love for him. You may get hurt, but at least you won't get left because he thinks you don't love him enough.

Many of my friends and patients have lost what they could have had because they bought into the myth that the best way to get what you want is to act as if you don't want it. I've heard people advise others to avoid asking someone if he has a lover when you first meet him, or even to hint that you want to move in with him before he suggests it. I've heard people say that treating other gay men with a bit of disdain keeps you mysterious, makes you look important, and encourages people to think of you as desirable, on the grounds that people who won't buy something for $2 will buy the same thing if it is priced much higher. Many gay men hear the advice that carefully crafted reticence, or creative disdain, is the order of the day because all gay men are afraid of intimacy, so pushing to get intimate will have the reverse effect. In truth, many gay men have accepted their need and desire for intimacy, they just don't know how to get as intimate as they might like.

The following incident occurred at a semi-gay restaurant where Hal, a personal friend, was eating. The tables are very close, and the man sitting behind him at the next table put his chair on top of Hal's raincoat, which Hal had draped over the back of his seat. When Hal got up to leave, he asked the man pleasantly if he could stand up so that Hal could retrieve his coat. As it happens, Hal is extrasensitive to nonverbal communications. He's often right, too, as he is a psychologist whose patients confirm the intuitive insights he has about them. He could just see the carefully crafted reticence in this man's demeanor, attitude, and body posture. It was as if the man were making a distance decision, and saying to Hal, with deliberate disdain, "Don't cruise me, you are too tired and not cute enough for handsome me. Of course I will give you your coat, just to be polite, but I don't want to be too friendly, because you might think I am interested in you, and I am not interested in you because I am too good, and too good-looking, for you." Now this man was good-looking, but not perfection himself. Besides, Hal wasn't cruising him; he was trying to retrieve his raincoat. In the meantime, Hal was saying to himself, "This is a good example of how readily people convey their off-putting feelings in nonverbal, but still apparent ways."

This incident illustrates my point that many gay men, trying to enhance their allure, actually push people away—and then complain that they cannot meet anybody. They use friendliness sparingly, as if it would kill them to be nice, warm, and inviting, as if it would somehow affect their self-esteem, because liking someone they deem to be inferior reflects poorly on them.

In my opinion, coy men may not become the objects of bidding wars as they hoped to be. Instead, they just might scare off gay men desiring intimacy, commitment, and monogamy. I believe that mutual dependency is a cornerstone of love, and as such is something to be nourished, not discouraged. There is nothing that discourages some men more than another man who is remote and unresponsive for whatever reason, including being independent or playing hard to get. Being independent and playing hard to get are good ways to be discourteous and cross signals. Wouldn't you rather lose someone after trying really hard than after pulling something cute and clever that backfired on you?

Meeting Mr. Right Is Not Really Your Goal

Although I speak of Mr. Right throughout this book, I only do so hypothetically and for my convenience. I still want you to do a reality check about looking for Mr. Right. Looking for Mr. Right immediately sets up a dichotomy. If someone is Mr. Right then presumably everyone else is Mr. Wrong. Instead of looking for Mr. Right, look for Mr. Middling. The world isn't so sharply divided into losers and winners. As with applying for a job, aim high but align your expectations to reality. Don't be too fussy. It's OK to pick and choose, but being too fussy tempts you to call everyone a loser, without actually bothering to evaluate the other person. Being adamant about who your "type" is limits you because types are preferences, and almost everybody has more than one of those.

I believe there is more than one man in the world for each of us. Many men could conceivably do. The idea that there is one right man for you—and one man only—is a fiction of love. It is not a bad fiction, but one nevertheless. When you are in love, you cannot imagine anyone else being right for you. But in reality, plenty of men would fill the bill.

Instead of looking for someone who is exactly right for you from the start, accept that people do grow, evolve, and change for each other—because they want to. No one is exactly right for anyone from the start. If you think they are, you will bypass a lot of good men with great potential. Joel, a personal friend, stopped drinking, cruising, and smoking for Michael, partly because he wanted to, and partly because Michael nagged him to until he did. Some people hate to be nagged, but Joel took Michael's nagging as proof that Michael loved him. Lovers change for each other all the time. That's why they call it love.

Optimistic men soon give up the conviction that little things mean a lot and avoid rejecting people outright because of this or that "little thing." For those serious about developing a relationship, a lot of things should mean little.

Bailing Out at the First Sign of Trouble Isn't a Good Idea

Instead of telling yourself, "Who needs this?" dig in even harder at the first sign of difficulty. Early relationship problems are not necessarily warnings of difficulties to come later. You have to go through a period of adjustment. Don't take a relationship for granted. Do what you can to make it work. Make the relationship come first, take it seriously, and devote as much time and thought to the budding relationship as you do to your cooking, clothing, or politics. Let nothing interfere—your work, family, or potential troublemakers. When there is a problem, like a fight, attempt to resolve your differences without acting on them. Don't flit to another relationship after condemning the whole of a new relationship just because one of its parts needs fixing.

Try making appropriate sacrifices for your new relationship. If necessary, be willing to give up something to get something, like your own gratification for the good of the relationship as a whole. Does he snore? Get a little less sleep. Does he drop clothes all over the floor? Play "pick up the sock." Change your identity too, within limits. Instead of suggesting, "Take me for myself or leave me be," be willing to make some compromises. Keep in mind that because perfection is not possible, imperfection is not a reason to move on.

Gay Life Doesn't Stop When You're Past Thirty

Don't panic if you are older, or newly widowed, divorced, or still unmarried. All is not lost. You can still find someone great. There are many men attracted to older people, for personal reasons, because they are attractive, or because they themselves are also older. You may be lovable because you are a father substitute, substituting for a father who was always remote. Or you may be attractive to those who prefer how older people look, or to those who prefer personality to looks, stability to immaturity, or predictability to the tumultuousness associated with prolonged adolescence.

If you have a problem with May-December marriages, it may not be a problem with the relationships themselves. Your problem may originate in a tendency to condemn all gay relationships on moral, sexophobic grounds, as in, "That's disgusting." If so, that is just another one of your guilt trips that has finally found a destination.

The Optimist's Creed

Committed gay relationships happen all the time. They work. They last. The sex gets better and better. You don't get restless, you just want the relationship to go on and on forever. In a relationship, your finances improve; you have the time, energy, and desire to be creative; your personality improves as you turn outside yourself to another person; and like all living things, you grow as you bask in the warmth, satisfaction, peace, and quiet of love. Tell anyone who tells you otherwise that they are wrong.

Now that you have successfully climbed Step Two, you know what's out there and are optimistic about your chances of finding it. The next step you have to climb is the one where you learn to avoid some of the pitfalls on your way to actually accomplishing your goal. In particular, before you can find Mr. Right you have to know who is Mr. Wrong, and steer clear of him.

3

Step Three: Avoid Mr. Wrong

In Step Three, you will learn how as a gay man you might wind up with unsuitable partners because of bad luck, inexperience, poor skills, a flawed or impractical approach to finding relationships, or impulsive, self-destructive tendencies that lead you to lose control, feel like hurting yourself, or make yourself be unsuccessful.

Common Reasons for Selecting Mr. Wrong

Keep in mind as you read through this list that my reasons are relative, not absolute, and that it's hard to predict with absolute certainty who is going to be Mr. Wrong for you.

Group Loyalty

Almost no one says, "I choose to be a small fish in a small pond," but that is exactly what you are doing if you are so devoted to a small group that you do not strike out on your own and find someone for yourself, someone right for you. In such cases, you let loyalty to your little group defeat you, because it becomes more important than consideration for yourself.

The groups that are particularly dangerous to your success are ones that have a selfish need to keep their individual members faithful to them. They know how to keep their members tethered to the group—discouraging any good relationship by invalidating your worth to him and his worth to you. They want you to get involved with Mr. Disaster so that they will have you back.

Judging by Looks Alone

Some men are cute—and that's about it. There's no denying it: cute gay men are much in demand. But for some gay men, looks are everything. They make lust choices, picking men strictly for appearance and the excitement that it brings. They go for a handsome man, not the person behind the pretty face, focusing on his youth, face, body, and major pecs—or his ability to look at home with that discus he appears to be getting ready to throw. Even some books on finding and keeping gay relationships seem to push a partner's good looks, if only indirectly. They picture a Mr. Right on the cover with a perfect bod and no clothes on. Having a gorgeous man who stays that way—frozen in time—is a universal fantasy. There are, however, many problems with it. Looks fade, and you need other things besides sex to sustain a relationship. That doesn't mean you should discard a good-looking man as a partner just because you lust for his bod. There is nothing wrong with choosing a handsome man. Just make sure that this isn't the only reason you like him, and that you will still like him when the initial attraction wears thin. If a relationship is to be sustained, other characteristics have to be there, too. Remember, sex only takes a couple of minutes (at most, ten times a day!), so you need something to do with the rest of your time.

Appearance was everything for one man I knew, Karl, from whom I heard, "He is so cute, I can forgive anything just because he has big, blue eyes and beautiful hair." Once, he picked a man primarily for his tresses, thinking himself in love with him because he loved his curls. I told Karl to watch it, and never to forget that in time looks invariably fade and off-putting personality problems tend to get worse. Therefore, if you pick a man for his looks and not his personality—and the relationship lasts—you run the risk that sooner or later you could be stuck with an ugly, miserable man.

In desperate situations, I give my patients a tongue-in-cheek assignment that actually works to stem the lust tide. When it is solely the construction boots and hard hat that grab you, call up a picture of your cute construction worker in your mind, and then add the following pin-ons in your imagination (or, if you are really ambitious, cutouts on the page): beer belly; scraggly beard; Monk's tonsure in front of the head as well as in the middle of the pate; can of beer in one hand and bag of potato chips in the other; newspaper on lap opened to the racing page; all comfortably ensconced, snoring perhaps, with mouth wide open and a little drool, in front of a television set tuned to the sports channel showing ten men running back and forth, back and forth, trying to put that ball into that basket. Paste these all on your image of loveliness, and at least you can save money on a crystal ball to tell you the trouble that you are getting yourself into.

Emotional Choices

An initial strong emotional reaction to someone can be one of the worst reasons to pick a partner. Almost by definition, people "in love" make emotional choices that fail to take important aspects of reality into account. Though this is only a general rule, try to supplement a feeling that starts from the crotch and goes to the brain with thoughts that start in the brain and go down to the crotch.

Trying to Impress Others

Pick someone who is right for you, not someone your friends will envy you for having snared. Forget the ego trip; the trip you want to be on is the one to the altar.

Christian wanted to be known by the fabulous company he kept. He had chosen a lover based on what the lover could do for his reputation. Christian didn't pick, he acquired a lover, and showed him off like he showed off his leather outfit and his God-given, naturally acquired cod piece. For him, there were no more important things in life than an admiring look from strangers as he passed by with his "humpy number" in tow, reveling in the USDA stamp of approval he got from others breathlessly validating the quality of his meat.

Men as Collectibles

You are trying to live a happy satisfying life, not, as the saying goes, trying to win by dying with the most toys.

Rolf seemed more interested in the number of notches on his gun than in the number of people he would be inviting to his wedding. He picked someone just to be able to add him to the ever-growing collection of trophies on his mantelpiece. I told him he deserved another trophy: my honorary cup for membership in an organization I created especially for Rolf and other gay men like him primarily interested in notching their guns: The NRA, or National Ruffle Association.

Men as Challenges

Challenge freaks feel that anything that comes easily cannot be any good, and the only man worth winning is the one you have to fight for. *That one over there wants you. Look, he is pointing the way to his blue BMW and asking you to get in and go with him for a ride off into the sunset.* What's the fun in that? *Look over there—there is someone much more interesting—that policeman on the nice horse. Feather in your cap if you can arrest him.*

Challenge freaks need to do things the hard way so that they can triumph over the odds and brag about it. They are like gamblers who become more interested in the game as their losses mount. They pursue relationships against greater and greater odds, and do double-or-nothings to make things whole. They also get caught up in vicious cycles where they take on harder and harder challenges as the need to create and overcome crises takes on a life of its own. This spurs them on to pursue relationships where the odds against success are greater and greater. They try to score bigger and better, both so that they can triumph over the odds and so that they can brag about their achievements. If you are one of these men, your mentality feeds on itself because it doesn't address the underlying problem, which is that you have to prove yourself big because you feel so small.

If you are one of these challenge-challenged men, stop what you are doing cold, pick up the pieces, go back to the beginning, and take an entirely new approach. Realize that the need to give yourself a handicap is itself your biggest handicap, and start doing things the easy way.

Spite Choices

Some people select a mate not because they love him or are trying to impress others, but to show someone, or show someone up. Perhaps they are trying to get back at someone for leaving them, or to come up even with friends who they think are better off. If this is the case, you are not choosing your lover so much as you are vanquishing your adversaries.

Envy, Perfectionism, and Fantasy

Envy is when you only want what someone else has, or something just like it. Men who choose mates out of envy do so based on someone else's apparent choices, not based on what is going to enhance their own lives.

A perfectionist's narrow vision fixes him on an ideal, making it difficult to compromise and consider men who do not exactly fit those criteria and requirements as partners. As a result of being a perfectionist, your dreams tend to be much more interesting than your reality.

Some gay men play games with themselves by indulging in fantasies about what the ideal life would be like, and some pick men to join them in making these fantasies a reality. The following is a list of common fantasies. Some of them are enjoyable, and some of them are fraught with danger. Whatever you do, don't use these fantasy scenarios to turn anyone down who doesn't fit them perfectly.

Boutique Fantasies

You and your lover retreat to a charming small town—preferably one on a small lake or large ocean—and open a little shop dealing with handmade crafts, and live the simple life together, arranging flowers in your florist's shop or whiling the time away whittling or making found objects into delightful, if somewhat overpriced, accessories.

Rescue Fantasies

You want to give a new lover all the advantages you had or never had, and to be all the things that you once were, or never were. You might pick a young lad without money and try to help him improve personally and professionally. You see your motivation as admirable, but one night he may run away back to his comfortable retreat living in the streets or at the "Y."

Osmosis Fantasies

Your lover becomes a source of strength for you to absorb, another phallus to supplement the one you already have. So you go for men who have all the qualities you wish you had. Problems arise if you find that these very qualities begin to grate on you because they are different from the ones you actually have (and don't dislike so much after all, which is why you have them in the first place).

Frank was a nervous-wreck type so he picked John because he liked the way John seemed unperturbed by all the "unnatural disasters" that befall gay men. At first, Frank wanted to become like John—so calm, so peaceful, such low blood pressure. That soon changed, however, as Frank began to look upon John as brain dead and wished he would react to something, anything, "like a normal human being who is still breathing."

Fantasies of Being Disciplined

You feel like a bad person and seek out a lover to put you over his knee and discipline you. You confess, and are cleansed, and now, ready, set, go, you are up and sinning all over again.

Twinning Fantasies

An extreme version of merger fantasies, this scenario involves dating someone exactly like you. These fantasies start with being close enough to use the same toothbrush and end up with applying to a surgeon to be joined at the hip.

Pygmalion Fantasies

Since love is blind, you don't have to give it an eye test. This fantasy involves shutting your lids and denying some really bad qualities about a potential partner, in the hope that you can change him. So what if he is unemployed; you can use your contacts to find him a job. So what if he is opportunistic; you are an opportunity.

Fantasies of Reparation

Some gay men have been so severely traumatized that they can never seem to get over it. For them, someone familiar from the past is the only thing that breeds present contentment. Compelled to repeat the past, they pick someone they can best repeat it with. To master their terrible early experiences, they recreate them over and over again, hoping or arranging for a new outcome this time around. Remote abusive mothers often create sons desperate for affection, precisely from those most likely to withhold it. These men really don't want affection, but want to find a stone to get blood out of.

If you recognize yourself in any of these descriptions, congratulations. You can now get to work recognizing when these subconscious conditions are acting to your disadvantage and leading you to make poor choices in partners. Meanwhile, there are also types of Mr. Wrong whom you might find yourself choosing over and over again.

The Mr. Wrongs of the World

The following are some examples of people who don't always make the best partners. Not only that, some of them can also interfere with your dating on a night-to-night basis. They get to you when you come to mingle in good faith, causing you to leave a broken thing, in your feelings, spirits, and heart. They corrupt your valid efforts and make life so unpleasant for you that you never want to go to a bar again, and you even hate being gay because of how other gay men treat you. I like to call these men "Attilas the Un"—the unavailable, the uninterested, the uninteresting, the unappetizing, the unacceptable, and the unwashed; and the mind-set in which you pick people like them is the State of Un-fatuation. In the discussion that follows, I sometimes spell out alternatives for you to consider, while at other times they are so obvious that I leave it up to you to figure out what they are. Also, if you see yourself in some of my examples, I ask you to make the necessary changes in your attitudes.

Promiscuous Men

Promiscuous men, like the man named Gary in the following example, are unavailable to you because their lives are too chaotic. They are too sexually pre-occupied to allow others to get close to them, and too busy to stop and commit to you—or to any other Mr. Right. They burn out by going to the bars Friday, drinking heavily, cruising until 4:00 A.M., meeting nobody, then repeating the process on Saturday and Sunday, getting no sleep for the whole weekend and dragging into work on Monday morning tired and hungover.

For Gary, promiscuity was extreme, unbalanced sex, an out-of-control behavior that preempted all other possibilities for now, and conditioned him to the point that changing over into commitment mode would be difficult to impossible later.

Gary spent entirely too much time in the bushes. In the early hours, the sun came up exposing a lean and hungry look on his face, the one predators have when they are still foraging about for a hit to keep them from going into emotional withdrawal.

Even upon meeting an available man, instead of saying hello, Gary still looked at everyone else, as if he didn't know where his next feel was coming from. Right from the start, Gary showed what kind of husband he would make: someone more interested in sex than in a relationship, someone who might have trouble making a commitment and sticking to it, someone unlikely to be faithful, and someone who would likely lose interest in a relationship completely as soon as the luster wore off the lust.

On those rare occasions when Gary had a partner for more than one night, he would come up with creative rationalizations to be able to continue being promiscuous without having to think of himself that way. He would normalize and legitimize promiscuity by building it into an "arrangement," so that he didn't feel promiscuous, but monogamous with exceptions—the ones, of course, that prove the rule. He would set up a number of limiting criteria detailing the frequency and type of sex that was OK before it crossed the line into unaccept-ability, limits like mutual masturbation no more than a few times a month and not on a weekend. As he saw it, these limits made "extramarital" sex acceptable by imposing artificial controls.

It's easy to criticize a man like Gary if you focus only on his behavior and on the effect he has on others. Don't forget how much pain he actually is in himself. His promiscuity was a source of personal guilt, and with it the lack of the self-respect he needed to create and maintain the respect, admiration, interest, and involvement of a lover. He thought of himself as a slut, then treated himself, and was treated in turn, just that way. Perhaps the worst of it is that Gary, like many promiscuous men, didn't even enjoy sex because the sex he had was missing intimacy, caring, and empathy. He was also wasting energy that he could have put to better use to create, maintain, and benefit an actual relationship. He threatened any relationship he got involved in by introducing an element of temptation into it.

Substance Abusers

Some men just drink too much. They fail to limit the amount of drinking they do in bars. I remember a time when I thought I had met this really great man. It was Christmas Eve, I was somewhat depressed about being alone, and I thought for sure my life was about to change. Unfortunately, come 3:00 A.M., my change of life passed out on the dance floor. In New York City, I could drink all I wanted to, so while I enjoyed myself drinking and dancing, I didn't meet as many people as I otherwise could have met. My own bar-cruising improved markedly when I went to places I had to drive home from, meaning I couldn't drink much while I was there.

Desperate Men

With these men, calm and self-control yield to flitting about in a way that makes you think you need a butterfly net to catch them. Desperate men have a problem with what I call "grabbadocio." While *braggadocio* is all about having too much confidence and telling everyone how wonderful you are, *grabbadocio* is all about having too little confidence, taking the first thing that comes your way, and thinking that it is more wonderful than it actually is.

Desperate men tend to grab the wrong person after fooling themselves into thinking that an inappropriate partner is a good catch. They don't check out the merchandise before buying. They do things impulsively, almost in a panic. They force a relationship in order to fill a void, only to discover that the more people they sleep with, the more their personal chasms yawn. James was just such a man, as the following story shows.

In a typical pattern, it's Saturday, the hour is getting late, it's last call, and the bar is closing, so James snags the first thing that looks available only to complain a few days later that the magic went out of the relationship. What James forgot was that the whole relationship was magic in the first place, because it was built entirely on an illusion.

Once James developed a passion for a scuzzy nurse's aide half his age, a relationship that everyone but James knew was unlikely to work. He even asked the young man to move in with him right in the middle of their first sexual encounter, when alcohol had heightened his sexual pleasure but dulled his judgment. Soon he got depressed when the boy started cheating on him—dragging men home when James was at work, and using James's apartment as a home base for selling drugs. By being desperate, James made a foolish and dangerous choice.

Disenfranchised and Disaffected Men

These gay men rebel against everything and everyone they consider to be square, uncool, and commitment-minded dullards. They have more sex than even they want to, as their way to tell the conservative, establishment-minded people pressuring them, "Get lost." Liking to be the exception that flouts all the rules, they won't pick you unless you are down and dirty enough to shock their mothers, someone they can bring home and announce, "Mother, meet my new husband, Prince Alarming."

Hustlers

Even the most suitable men want something real from you and from the relationship, so it's not always easy to tell when someone crosses the line from rustler to hustler. I urge you to at least try to spot the obvious cases, and not get too involved before figuring out if he wants your life or your money.

Ronald was a man other men enjoyed for his earthy qualities, that is, he was dirt. He worked at the baths, occasionally emerging from the vapors to meet a new patron when the last one's patience or money ran out, and not necessarily in that order. Speaking of the waters, he used men's to fish in, finally depleting their stock with all his needs and demands. He was one of those people to whom my aphorism applies: "Feed a man and he will eat for a day. Teach a man like Ronald to fish and he will eat the bait."

Bitchy Queens

This is an archetype in gay circles, and unfortunately it's also some people's type. You have no doubt run across the classic bitchy queen. He is that man who dished you until it hurt. He had fun dishing you, but his fun was at your expense, and he didn't exactly win you over.

Frank is a classic bitchy queen, someone to steer clear of unless you want to spend the rest of your life in steerage. Frank went to gay bars not to find love but to pick a fight. He would be full of anger at a particular gay man, at the whole process of dating, or at gay life in general. Sometimes his rage was disguised as boredom, but mostly it was pretty obvious, and he made no attempt to spare others its effects.

In bars, Frank did not say hello when he was introduced to people. He affected an air of disdain copied from a waiter at a prominent gay restaurant, a man who could smile and insult you at the same time. Frank felt that was sexy.

Frank also badmouthed people behind their backs. Frank met Ralph, a handsome man with a big country home, tons of money, two handsome dogs, and lots of love. But instead of appreciating Ralph, he refused to see Ralph again because he had a minor physical deformity. He told everyone in the bar about it too, even people who knew Ralph, thought he was cute, and wanted him themselves.

People who overheard Frank being critical of others knew they were next and decided they didn't want an insult comic for a partner. As a result, many of the men Frank called creeps became partners of someone else.

Passive-Aggressive Men

Passive-aggressive men hurt subtly and indirectly. They act out their problems with dependency, control, and competition through petty vengeances, leaving their victims thinking that it was something they did that brought on the unpleasantness. Refusing to commit, being late, and teasing are common passive-aggressive behaviors that turn the mating game into the baiting game.

Arnold dragged his feet and couldn't or wouldn't commit to Stewart. Stewart should have recognized that Arnold had a commitment problem when, on the first night they were together, Arnold excused himself for a moment and disappeared for an hour. Later in the relationship, Arnold did promise Stewart commitment, and in all fairness moved in that direction, but at a snail's pace. First, Stewart begged Arnold to tell his family about him—and Arnold obliged, finally, a year later. Then Stewart begged Arnold to get him a ring—and Arnold did, six months later, telling Stewart to be sure to hang on to the receipt. Then Stewart begged Arnold to set the date for moving in with him, and he said he would and even set a date not too far off into the future, but then he missed the deadline. Then Arnold did move in with him and agreed to have a commitment ceremony, but he forgot to schedule the hall and hire the caterer.

A great deal of gay misery results from passive-aggressive insults, dallying, withholding, shifty commitment, and the like. Of course, this isn't strictly a gay problem. Such abusive behavior can affect any kind of relationship, gay or straight. An important principle here is that not all misery of gays is gay misery. Just because you are gay doesn't mean you cannot be a victim of ordinary abuse, for abuse doesn't discriminate according to sexual orientation.

Married Men

Unfortunately, it is necessary to remind some gay men that one of the most common bad choices gay men make is to choose someone who is already taken. It is surprising how many gay men, even though they know that most married men have no intention of leaving their wives or husbands and committing to them, still go with a married man, fooling themselves into believing that this time it will be different and they will be the exception.

Gay men who go with married men almost always play the mistress to the household, and they suffer endlessly as days and nights alone follow days, and rarely nights, together.

Why do gay men do this? First, many gay men choose married men because they are in reality very attractive. Others choose married men because they have a lottery mindset: maybe your chances of winning aren't great, but the payoff is so good that the chance is worth taking. For other men, it is the lottery challenge: you only want to play the games that are hard to win, because if you win it makes you feel so much better about yourself, so much more potent. It is as if now you can do anything, and who knows what you might accomplish next.

Some gay men like men who are already taken. Their attached status puts the stamp of approval on them, along the lines of, "What I've got must be good because someone else wants it." Some people are happiest when they make a third party—the partner the married man already has—unhappy. Others don't stop to think of all the difficulties involved, or think they are so wonderful, or adept, that they can surmount them. Still others don't care that he is already taken—they are so much in love that they continue the pursuit anyway.

If you seem to be showing a preference for married men take this short quiz.

Question: Why are married men unmarriageble?

Answer: Because they are already married.

You passed the quiz if you answered that question correctly and didn't act in the past—and won't act in the future—as if the answer doesn't apply in your case. Also ask yourself these questions:

- Does he just want a mistress?
- Do you feel you are so wonderful that he will give up a long-term, functional relationship to be with you?
- Does your passion mean you don't care if he ever loves you, or if he never loves you exclusively?

One or more "yes" answers means say "no" to the relationship.

If you need any additional reasons to avoid such a relationship, I advise you that:

- Many married men are just using you to increase their self-esteem or to help them get revenge on a present husband or wife.
- Going after a married man is a form of distancing behavior where you fool yourself that you tried, while making sure that you haven't succeeded.
- If a married man is what you want, go ahead and try to get one, but accept the consequences graciously, because you brought them on yourself—foolishly.
- Either avoid trouble, or get into it and keep quiet. It is unacceptable to court trouble and then complain when it marries you.

Don't get involved with a married man unless he is truly separated or divorced and is emotionally over that relationship. A lover who is already married, complains about his wife or husband, and says that he plans to leave her/him and will marry you as soon as the divorce comes through is unacceptable unless he does just what he says he will do, and does it yesterday. Two things are worth having before you pursue that relationship one more minute: his divorce decree and your marriage proposal.

Perhaps you are currently involved with a married man and cannot give him up. At least be sensible about your relationship. Don't let it drag on endlessly while your life ebbs as his flows. In the meantime, cheat on him—fair is fair and he is cheating on you. Better still: cheat on him with someone single. That's your way out.

Men Who Are Not Interested in You

Some gay men, forgetting to ask, "What does he really want from me?" choose someone who is disinterested in them, only to be disappointed when the relationship doesn't work out.

Tom, a much older man, once made this mistake with an eighteen-year-old user who said that he loved him, but who really wanted a place to live, a perch from which he could meet a real lover, not one, to quote the boy, who was "too old." The boy did meet a real lover and fled from Tom's home on some jerrybuilt excuse. What should have been Tom's first clue that there was a problem? Two weeks after the boy moved in he received a letter from a new admirer. Certified mail.

Climbing Step Three saves you a lot of grief in the way of wrong turns and interpersonal disasters that leave you panting for less. I don't want you to artificially limit your choices, but I do want you to stay away from men who are really bad news. You now know who they are and are ready to climb the next step. When you have climbed that, you will be high enough to be able to spot Mr. Right over the heads of the crowd.

4

Step Four: Pick Mr. Right

General Rules
Here are some good mind-sets to have and attitudes to guide you as you search for Mr. Right.

Be Flexible
Adjust your expectations. Rate men on an ascending scale from zero to ten, then, realizing how many good things come in ordinary packages, consider picking numero zero. On one hand, expect the most wonderful things to happen. On the other hand, realize that the most ordinary things can be the most wonderful.

Don't Prejudge Relationships
It is generally difficult to anticipate what relationships will and what relationships will not work out. Relationship planning is an inexact science. Premarital compatibility studies, like rules for determining the direction of the stock market, are not inclusive enough to predict the future with any degree of accuracy. Exogamous, where you favor men as unlike you as possible, endogamous, where you favor men who resemble you a great deal, or any other kind of relationships can work out or fail, depending on many factors. If my patient Mark's relationship worked, after starting out purely as a spite relationship, as an attempt

to hurt a former lover by becoming lovers with his best friend, then any relationship can survive it's own initial premise. A partnership is like a creative writing project. So often you have nothing much to say in the beginning, but everything pours out once you get started.

How matched should two men ideally be? Not very, one way or the other. Instead of trying to literally make a match, fall in love with someone without making his age, race, or other superficial qualities too important. Truly basic, really lovable qualities exist in different men of various types. Some of the best relationships satisfy a little bit of both paradigms: opposites attract, and so do birds of a feather. To make a successful couple, the individuals don't have to be alike and they don't have to be different. They just have to learn what they can from each other and from their differences, and move on from there.

Frank's lover Ty is like Frank, one of my patients, in some ways. They have similar interests, for example they both like New York. They also differ in certain key respects—Ty is Jewish and Frank is black. Ty doesn't like to go to contemporary music concerts, Frank enjoys them. Ty likes lithographs of abstract squares, Frank prefers abstract squiggles. There are key personality differences, too—Ty is very relaxed, Frank is very uptight. Ty wants to see what will happen before worrying about it, Frank wants to worry about it before he sees what is happening. Frank learns from Ty: he worries about an upcoming tax bill less when Ty says, "It is what it is and we will just have to make adjustments." Ty learns from Frank: following Frank's example, Ty goes to the dentist twice a year to check his teeth in case he should get a cavity.

Remember that as relationships progress and develop, superficial characteristics matter less and less.

Be Motivated

It is the motivation to make a relationship work that makes all the difference. Motivation makes all the seemingly important initial similarities and differences secondary.

Put Love in Perspective

Don't do what you love, love what you do. Love may come first, or it may come later after the two of you are partners for a while, and have made that partnership work.

Love is not the only reason to get married any more than doing what you love is the only reason to pick a career. Make practical choices. Consider picking not the men who excite you but the men who make you think about checking the address of city hall, where the two of you can go to get that marriage license.

Look Around at What You Already Have

This approach is so shocking and revolutionary, you may not believe it, but you'd be surprised at how often this one simple approach works. Ready? Here it is: take a second look at what you already have. Don't have a lover? Maybe you do—only you don't know it yet. Carl, one of my patients, knew his for seven years, as a friend, before "it" happened. Carl put his emotional conflicts on a back burner, took another peek at the single-room occupancy that symbolized his existence, and, being practical for once in his life, reevaluated Matt, someone he had known for years but had not previously considered a romantic possibility. They offered each other a ride off into the sunset together. That was about twenty years ago and the music for the credits is still playing today.

Select, Then Settle

Whatever the nature of the original choice, usually making some choice is better than not making any choice at all. Bad choices don't work out, but I believe that the pain of separation is less than the pain of isolation. That's another reason why it is not a good idea to make the conditions too strict for choosing your partner of a lifetime.

Some Good Qualities

Because the good qualities you expect in him interlock with the ones he expects in you, this list should be used in conjunction with the list of good qualities you would want to develop in yourself that I present in Step Seven. You'll want to both develop these qualities in yourself as well as seek them in another:

1. **Sincerity.** He doesn't play games. He is ready to have a relationship.

2. **Interest.** You are his first choice, not someone who comes after his wife or present husband or the lover he really wants but cannot have or his dog or his apartment or his bank account or his clothes or his casual sex partners.

3. **Stability.** He has a job and either lives with his parents or roommates or has his own place to live. His address isn't the streets and (as happened to me once) he isn't one of the stable boys of an older man who is presently offering room and board to runaways in exchange for sex.

4. **Motivation.** He wants to iron out the kinks in a relationship, not throw away the relationship because it is imperfect.

5. **Potential.** The present reality may be questionable but the possibilities for the future seem infinite.

6. **Intelligence**. He knows what you are talking about and says a few things you don't already know. If he didn't get an advanced degree in school, at least he is talented, good with his hands, or possessed of a special, perhaps artistic, bent and ability.

7. **Flexibility.** He is open to what he wants and accepting of what you have to give him. He accepts "no" both as an answer and as a suggestion.

8. **Lack of serious inhibitions.** He isn't all tied up in knots personally or sexually.

9. **Lack of serious disinhibitions.** He doesn't drink heavily, smoke the bad stuff, and isn't sexually promiscuous, or if he is, is ready to give that up right now.

10. **Exclusiveness.** He may have eleven snapshots left on the film, but he stops shooting and has the roll developed after he takes your picture.

11. **Humor.** He doesn't go into orbit if you happen to say the wrong thing but laughs it off instead, or at least gives you a chance to explain yourself.

Some Qualities That Don't Matter

Here is a short list of things that don't matter much in a potential partner:

1. **Pedigree.** In my opinion, his background doesn't matter at all. I myself was always particularly fond of men who are salt-of-the earth types, you know, the kind without much pretense. They were great themselves, and they always had such interesting, and often warm and caring, families.

2. **Looks.** He can be cute but he doesn't have to be. After a while, you will not even notice what he looks like. Besides, cute is strictly a subjective evaluation, one almost entirely in the eye of the beholder.

3. **Money and possessions.** Give up envying men with large houses and complete collections of anything. The happiest couple I know lives, without a sou to their names, in a trailer park—and they have been living there for forty years.

4. **Family background.** It's nice to have in-laws you get along with, but it's not necessary. You can make your own little nuclear family, and as long as you have each other you will always have a place to go for the holidays.

5. **Friends.** Don't necessarily pick a man because you like the social circles he travels in. Some gay couples are very social; others are much more limited in their contacts, with just a few selected friends. Many of my patients found that being very social raised some definite problems for their relationships, especially in the beginning. The cross-cruising was intense, and sometimes there was backstabbing too. Many friendships don't survive a new relationship—as old friends feel the loss of a buddy, feel left out of the action, resent your success, or like one of you better than the other.

You have now climbed Step Four—congratulations to you. Now you know what you want from a relationship, the truth about what relationships have to offer, and who is and who isn't in a position to give you what you want. You can stop to catch your breath here, but I suggest you go on to Step Five immediately. Here you will learn where your Mr. Right lives and what doors to knock on to get him to answer. Some of my suggestions are obvious, but some will surprise you, either because you haven't thought of them before or because you did but thought that they weren't right for you. The suggestions in Step Five might very well help you get out of a cruising rut and expand your horizons. I learned about this step when, after haunting the discos night after Saturday night without anything happening, I finally decided, "This is ridiculous, there must be life after the boogie," and began to haunt the houses where there were real people just waiting to believe in me.

5

Step Five: Where to Go to Find Him

Now that you have taken Steps One through Four—deciding on having a relationship, taking a look at the myths and realities of relationships, learning to avoid Mr. Wrong, then learning how to pick Mr. Right, you are ready for Step Five, going out and finding him.

General Principles

Learning where to go to find Mr. Right starts with mastering a few simple general principles.

All You Need Is One Man

One of the greatest reasons for love problems among gay men is the feeling that they have to be very popular to be loved, and they are not popular unless they are surrounded by a circle of admirers.

You Can Meet Men Wherever You Are and Whenever You Go There

In my experience, many long-lasting love affairs started in the least likely places, not in gay bars but in department-store aisles, or at parties that were supposed to be straight. My own relationship started in my living room. Charles, a good friend, discovered that you can meet Mr. Wonderful anywhere. Charles used to go regularly to a seedy gay hotel on Long Island. Others said they wouldn't be caught dead there. But that's exactly where Charles found the catch of his life.

Even though some places are primarily places to go for sex, it is still possible to meet men there for a committed relationship. Some gay men, in fact, make it a practice to go to these places to try to find lovers. They go there in part because that's where the gay men are, and in part because they like the thought of converting men who are wild cruisers into men who are stable homebodies, converting sinners into saints, rescuing men from themselves by offering them a chance to settle down. I have no personal knowledge of successful relationships that started in these places, and I don't necessarily recommend them, but at least theoretically there is no reason that they can't work out. I do know that some of the best husband material consists of the man who is going through a promiscuous phase but is uncomfortable with it and just scouting for a lifeline out. People change all the time, and the way a relationship starts says very little about its prospects. I consider it very likely that people have met their husbands at the baths, the rest stops, the men's rooms in college libraries, the back rooms of bars, the bushes, pornographic movie houses, and gay bookstores. They may not be the land of promise, but they can be the land of opportunity. To a great extent, it depends upon the morality and flexibility of the individuals involved, and that includes a willingness not to hold anything from his past against a possible future partner. I met a very close friend at a bar of very ill repute, and while we didn't become lovers, we could have in other circumstances. He had plenty of friends he introduced me to who would have made good lovers if I hadn't gone off in another direction.

No place is completely straight either. If you sort places into straight and gay, you will just cruise summertime in Provincetown, put your antennae down, close your mind, and forget about trying to connect during wintertime in the suburbs. Instead, try hard to make it outside of as well as inside of the gay ghettos. It's actually quite hard trying to make it in gay ghettos. These are some of the many reasons why it's easier than you think to meet someone in laundromats and supermarkets than it is in the Castro section of San Francisco. In gay ghettos, there's too much competition, expectations usually run too high to be fully met, self-homophobia and the cruising guilt it engenders float to the top because the situation is so highly charged erotically, and you never know which one of hundreds of possible men to choose.

You can meet men in a straight town; a straight part of a semi-gay town, like the scenic walk; a boat cruise on a straight boat; or a video store. While cruising low-yield, non-cruising places takes patience, the rewards are often proportionate. Mel, a middle-aged gay friend who would like to be married but so far has had no luck at it, was ensconced in an outdoor cafe in a straight part of the Village with his food, glass of wine, and Sunday *Times* crossword puzzle. He continued to scowl as he worked the puzzle and drank the wine, thinking, "I am looking for someone, but gay men don't go to straight touristy sections of New York, therefore I cannot meet anyone here, so why bother trying." Instead of making the most out of where he was, Mel usually made it a point to only cruise places where the cruising yield might be high, so instead of concentrating on what he was doing today he dreamed about heading off for weekends in Provincetown, or Fire Island Pines, or some other gay ghetto where he thought he could have the best chances and the greatest success. Mel did meet men there, but he could have met them right where he was, places where there was less danger in numbers due to intense competition, and less of a party mentality that danced away the night, along with his chances.

Ed, Mel's opposite, was another gay friend who had met no one in the bars or on the gay beach in Ogunquit, Maine, a semi-gay resort, after ten years of trying. Eventually, I convinced him to stop depending on the bars and the gay beach exclusively to search for a lover, and to also walk the Marginal Way, an ocean-front path, during the day. It was there that Ed finally met his lifetime lover.

When you look for love isn't important either. Some gay men only look for love at night. If you do that, your mind will be closed to meeting men at some of the best times to meet them—like morning in the city or in the subway on your way to work.

It's a Good Idea to Look for Love All of the Time

The most productive looking is continuous and unfocused, not just limited to certain times and places. Gay men who are only intermittently available for love often outsmart themselves by becoming too intense, too concentrated, and too focused in their endeavors. Fortunately, looking for Mr. Right is one of the few full-time jobs you can do while you are otherwise fully employed.

Don't Waste Your Time in Certain Places

A few places can actually be a waste of time. Places where it is dark don't offer much. Sex in the dark is by definition strictly anonymous, and means to stay that way. Certain places mostly cater to voyeurs who are there to look and idealize, not to meet a real person. You can meet people in such places but in some respects it's like trying to find a ballet lover at the rodeo. You might find one, but you will most likely just be battling insurmountable odds.

Focus on Going to Triple-Threat Places

Places like the public library are great because they allow you to enjoy yourself, be personally productive, and have a reasonable chance of meeting someone special all at the same time. Enjoy where you are first. A particular benefit of such places is that they let you go to sleep early, before the late bar closings that keep you up all night and from looking as good tomorrow as you look today.

Be Aware of Your Signals

A single man who goes out to dinner alone to a gay restaurant won't meet anybody if he doesn't signal his availability. Surrounding yourself with an invisible shield of newspapers will only send a signal that you are not available or not looking.

Specific Suggestions

Here are a number of specific places you can go to meet a lover. This list is incomplete, and it can also be a good idea to be a contrarian who does the exact opposite of what I, or anybody else, suggests. As a contrarian, you might make a list of all the places I left out or tried to steer you away from, then go there too, or first. Go to the town recycling center. Go down to the docks where the fishing boats are (not those docks).

Gay Recreational Establishments

Gay summer camps, gay boat cruises, and the semi-gay resorts in your area are great places to cruise for love. Only sign up for a long vacation at a gay resort or on a gay boat cruise if you like the destination and will not be disappointed if you don't meet someone nice. Vacations are different from bars. You have more investment in a boat cruise than you do in a night in the bar, so only go if you enjoy traveling and won't be devastated if nothing happens. Don't allow misleading advertisements to lure you in, either. The models they photograph on the cruise boat you are thinking of taking are, in real life, not on your boat but on someone's private yacht.

Gay and Lesbian Centers

These are excellent places to go, in many ways better than all the others on my list. Don't think people have to be desperate to go there either. Thinking that just gives you a jaundiced view of who you might meet in such places. Even if you are desperate, it doesn't mean that you, or they, are a desperate case. It just means that you are lonely for now, and sooner or later that can happen to anybody, even the greatest among us.

Straight (as well as Gay) Parties

Never say early in the evening at a straight party, "There is no one cute here. Let's blow this joint and go out to the clubs." Maybe what you want isn't here—but he could just be waiting elsewhere to be introduced to you by someone who is at the party. Stay and mingle until the party is over; you can always go out later.

Straight Bars, Baseball Games, and the Races

A lot of men who go to straight bars, baseball games, or the races are closet cases who like being with other men but don't admit it to themselves, and certainly don't think of themselves as gay or available. Some of the men there are overcompensating by acting very straight. Maybe you can help them decompensate, back to what they really want. There is danger in bringing "straight" men out, because some of them will resent and blame you for it, and attack you for your efforts. However, some "straight" men can be had with a little push, and they can make good husbands when they tip, after they get over their reluctance and the shock of self-realization. This approach is very risky. Be prepared for a lot of emotional baggage if you take this route. It is not that it doesn't have its rewards. I just want you to be careful.

Outdoor Cafes and Other Restaurants, Straight or Gay

Many lonely gay men simply refuse to eat out alone, and their friends reinforce that attitude by saying, "It's humiliating to ask for a table for one." A gay man who used to be that way after many years gave a straight restaurant a try one particular night when he had nothing better to do. He didn't meet his lover there, but he did meet some nice people, partly because he got the sympathy vote as people came up to him after dinner to tell him that they had been there and done that, and sympathized with what he was going through. One of them even introduced him to the man who was to become his lifetime lover.

The Streets—No, Not Those Streets

Walk everywhere and look for Mr. Right everywhere you walk. This works particularly well if you do more than just walk and gawk, and especially if you initiate that smile and say hello back to someone who looks at you deeply, and/or twice.

Synagogues, Churches, Mosques, and the Like, Gay and Straight

There are gay church groups and gay churches and synagogues (and other houses of worship) available to you. Certain straight churches and synagogues also attract and encourage a gay clientele. Many gay men hesitate to make use of these facilities because they feel they have to be very religious to attend, or because they feel especially sinful under the eyes of God. In my experience, it is truly amazing what can happen even when Someone is watching.

AA and Group Therapy

Don't get sick just to attend sessions and don't attend sessions if you are not sick, but if you are sick and need the treatment, go looking for more than just a cure. Be sure to leave the group if it isn't working for you therapeutically. For example, you might get depressed if others in the group are so depressed that they bring you down.

Video Stores

People who go to video stores are often alone and eager to meet someone, which is why they are renting videos on Saturday night in the first place. I believe that straight video stores offer a much better yield than pornographic video stores, but there is no reason you cannot try the latter if you are so inclined. Just don't set your mind to believing that the nonpornographic video stores are for entertainment, while the pornographic video stores are for meeting men and for in-house sex.

Chinese, or Other Take-Out Restaurants

Never have your food delivered. Always pick it up yourself. You might pick up more than you bargained for. Many single men eat out alone in Chinese restaurants. There is less of a stigma eating out alone in an informal setting than there is in the more formal settings of other restaurants. That makes eating in at Chinese restaurants another high-yield possibility.

The Laundromat

Have a washer and dryer in your apartment building or in the basement of your house? Don't use it. Make those quarters do double duty—for cleaning your clothes, and for paying your way for your stay in a public place full of bachelors. People also tend to do their laundry when they are off for the evening, and are receptive because they are relaxed, not rushed, and it's still early.

The Gym

My patients met more men in the gym than anywhere else, except bars. You can too, and it's pretty obvious why. First, there is the locker room. Unless this is a gay gym, the cruising has to be very subtle here. The floor of the gym is a much better place to actually flirt than the locker room. There are a thousand reasons to start a conversation here, like, "Are you through with the machine?" or, "How do you do this exercise?" Watch those gym clothes—too fancy is usually less appealing than simple and rough, with designer gym outfits tending to look like your psychotherapist prescribed them. Again, pay particular attention to your sneakers—they appeal to gay men (a large number) with a sense of style. Tight clothes are out unless you can really do them justice. Good form during your workout is as sexy as good form in the ballet. The gym is a great place to network if you do it right. The same people go to the gym day after day, giving you an opportunity to develop a little coterie. I have, however, observed a number of people forming cliques whose purpose seems to be as much to exclude as to include others. My impression is that the excluded ones are looking on in anguish, just wanting a little kind word and some recognition, just waiting there for you to say hello and include them in the festivities. These people are a wonderfully unrecognized lode for you to mine. Some gyms have coffee shops where you can hang out—another place to find a lonely Mr. Wonderful. Here's a triple-threat idea. First go to the gym, then pick up some Chinese food, then after dinner go to a gay and lesbian center.

Funerals, and the Cemeteries after the Funeral

Don't push too hard here. That's a little macabre. Still, if you can get past that, funerals, especially after the ceremony, are as much a celebration of life as they are a mourning for the dead—why else would people eat so heartily at the wake? The lover of the deceased may not be fair game for now, but his friends certainly are. And keep him in mind for later. A year from now you might just be what he needs to help him get over his grief.

Volunteering at a Soup Kitchen

AIDS organizations such as Housing Works, Meals on Wheels, and your block association all harbor great opportunities. Gay men do fall in love with people they work with. Volunteering at a soup kitchen gives you the chance to meet men and do a good deed at the same time. Plus, the vicarious pleasure you get from helping others will only make you more eager and receptive to getting something for yourself. The iron is hot, so strike.

Cooking Class

In my experience, many single men try this knowing that it is a high-yield place to meet a lover, and not just leftovers either. Many therapists advise their single patients to take a cooking class. So, you not only have a captive audience, you also have one that is highly motivated to make the class really cook.

Stores

The record store is a good place to try. High yield: the classical and dance music sections. For specialists: the ethnic music sections. Home furnishing and kitchen stores are another great place to look for love. Follow the single men furnishing their houses—maybe you'll be one of the items they pick up. Bookstores with coffee shops and library-like reading areas are great too. High yield: the gay studies sections. Department stores are particularly good, especially in the designer clothing departments, as are supermarkets after work, where you might consider asking him how to cook a chicken or braise a veggie. Out-of-town supermarkets can be even better. One trick that sometimes works for city people is to stay with a friend who lives in the suburbs and go food shopping with him. You are a new face, and the people there are old homebodies, often both desirable and desperate. Shop the local supermarkets around 5:50 P.M., the time when divorced and unmarried men are just getting off work and picking up dinner (and perhaps you).

Art Gallery Openings

They're free, and so is the wine and cheese. The crowd at these openings tends to be very intellectual, very gay, very smart, and, when by themselves, very lonely. As with cooking class, you have a receptive audience because many of them are actually going there to meet new people, having been told it's a good place to try. The paintings on the wall make a great conversation piece. Just avoid saying things like, "I could have done that myself, and in kindergarten. I cannot believe that anyone would actually pay for a black canvass with a little white spot in the corner." That has been said before, and saying it again just makes you look unappreciative and repetitive. A better remark: looking at a million-dollar painting, you might say that it's worth buying just for the frame.

The Theatre, Concerts, and Other Entertainments

Many of these are high-yield places for specialists, like opera buffs, people interested in the theatre or ballet, and the like. Try to go on a week night—that's when all the single men are out because they have nothing better to do, or have decided that they don't care that they are alone, they just want to see the show. There are some gay shows with a predominantly gay audience, and you might try these too.

The Ferry or Train to Gay or Semi-gay Resorts

No one says you actually have to have a house at a gay resort to go there. Go for the day. The trip out can be as rewarding as the arrival, and even better. You can virtually pick the kind of man you like, too, as you choose the ferry to the island, or the train to the country. Don't sell the bus short either. My bus trips to Maine produced some interesting possibilities.

Paducah, Kentucky, and Fall River, Massachusetts

Too many gay men concentrate on big cities and gay towns in the mistaken belief that no gay people live in small and straight towns. When they go to small/straight towns, they lower their "antennae" and turn off their "radio." From what I see in the town we live in, what is supposed to be a small redneck area of New Jersey, plenty of gay dating goes on—and either I am really great or they are really desperate. You can even try the malls. Particularly in small towns, gay men have no other place to go.

In Your Own Living Room

If you are giving a party and someone asks, "Can I bring so and so?" always answer, "Yes." Invite as many popular people as you know over. Eventually, one of them will ask to drag someone along to your place. That's how I met Michael. His friend from school, my lover at the time, asked if he could bring him along. There was only one condition: I had to promise not to laugh. Apparently his friend, my lover, thought that he was doing Michael a favor by knowing him and introducing him to someone who wasn't an animal.

A good idea is to have an annual party, like a Christmas party for people who have no place else to go. You develop a good reputation in certain circles of lonely gay men, and a following, too.

In Your Cousin the Matchmaker's Living Room

Forget the negative myths about matchmakers. Meeting a lover through mutual friends often works and has many advantages, too. It's a good way to meet other members of an establishment you are hopefully planning to become part of.

The Recycling Center

In some suburbs at least, everybody has to go here eventually. The recycling center is a great place to bump into and meet the men who live in your neighborhood, especially the environmentally conscious ones. Here's a good trick: if you spot someone interesting, note the time and day, and return there the same time next week. Chances are that he is on a schedule and you might see him again and again—a great opportunity for a recognition scene.

The Real Estate Section of Your Newspaper

Some people put in, or answer, ads for apartments to share. They do this not because they need a place to live but to meet someone they hope to eventually live with. Just because some people do it for sex doesn't mean that you cannot do it for love.

The Personal Ads

Personal ads for relationships are found in gay and straight newspapers and on the Internet. (I am speaking of ads for relationships, not for sex.) You hear many things about the personal ads, most of them bad, but many of the things you hear are myths. It is very easy to get down on the ads and the people you meet in them. So, if you are reading and thinking about responding to ads, cut them some slack and give them a try.

Sometimes, the ads themselves include a number of turnoffs—mostly unintended. If you can read between the lines, and sense it's a case of nervousness or guilt about asking for what the writer really wanted, why not give it a try? Nothing ventured, nothing gained.

As everyone knows, the personals can be dishonest. Some ad writers bend key truths and leave out key unmentionables. One of the most dishonest aspects of some of these ads is when someone attempts to disguise that what they really want is a cute humpy number, as in, "Sincere, kind person wanted for meaningful long-term, committed, sharing relationship, age 18–22, no fats no femmes no farmers, and, of course, picture please because physical attraction is important, no matter what people say." It is hard to suppress the suspicion that such a person is looking for a cute man for a one-night stand, and waving the carrot of committment just to get at your stick.

Some people use the personals as a fantasy or ego trip. A gay patient told me that, "In my opinion, the personals are like the boutiques in a certain chic summer resort I go to. The people who run these boutiques love to set them up. They have many boutique fantasies, all starting with the word "lovely" and ending with the word "delightful." In their fantasies, Gordon Lightfoot is usually singing 'If You Could Read My Mind Love' in the background on a small portable radio. Perfumed candles are lit in anticipatory celebration of the hordes about to descend. However, when the crowds actually arrive, the owner experiences not joy but grief. Now reality intrudes and he or she gives up on the whole thing and cannot wait to shut down for the winter. I once was that way with the personals. I used them to discharge fantasy, forgetting that they are meant to be reality. When the under-par candidates arrived, I got impatient and closed up shop, pushing all those potentially good customers out into the cold."

Yes, these things are all true about the personals. But also true is that, used appropriately, the personal ads can be another tool in your expanding toolbox newly brimming with gadgets that can help you fix what is broken.

If you are writing ads, express your legitimate needs and desires honestly in a passionate but realistic way. Be empathic. Think of how you would respond if you were reading your own ad. Be practical, too. Some of the best ads contain the following simple but direct statements—things most people can deal with:

- No luck yet.
- As a person I am not great but not bad either.
- Let's give it a try, what do we have to lose?

Put these ideas in your own words, without layers of pretense that promise something larger than life.

Avoid being superficial, emphasizing such relatively meaningless "positive" attributes as a preference for yellow candles and walks on the beach at night—things that trivialize you, prompting others to do the same and think of you as an insubstantial person, or a phony.

When people answer your ad, try out as many of the candidates who respond as you possibly can. When reading their letters, remember that a book often differs from, and can be considerably better than, its cover.

Avoid being self-destructive. After writing a great ad, Patrick, a patient I was seeing in long-term therapy, threw away all the potentially good responses and instead glommed onto those people who intrigued him the most—the ones with personal problems. Needing a man like his rejecting mother, he picked critical and unavailable people, discarding all others. For example, he didn't respond to someone who said he had a second job as a clown because he was convinced that to be a clown you must be a clown, that is, a moron. But convinced that big muscles made the best embrace, he eagerly expressed interest in a man who did seven hundred pushups a day, overlooking all the obvious clues that he was a mean and nasty person, which it turned out he was.

Be honest about yourself. Don't try to comb your flaws over. What you lose by being open about yourself, and your possible problems, you gain by being truthful. Truth appeals to someone looking for a relationship, not a one-night affair. The truth will come out anyway, and when it does, elaborations will be exposed—not something likely to advance your cause or enhance your reputation in a world where, especially when it comes to exchanging inside knowledge about others' flaws, it at least seems as if everyone knows everyone else.

Try not to get involved in an uncomfortable and draining situation, let alone one that is dangerous. A patient of mine agreed to go all the way to the Philippines for a liaison on the basis of a photograph of a man whose face was very pretty. However, the man hid his tiny stature using trick photography, and when my patient saw him he knew that all the money and time devoted to the trip was wasted.

In conclusion, I advise using personal ads, but using them wisely. Using the personals is just another method of selling yourself effectively and buying what is good and available. As with mining for gold, there are nuggets among the dross. With a little bit of luck and a lot of persistence, and if you can avoid being too easily discouraged and acting self-destructively, you may find what you are looking for.

However, if you give the personals a try, don't make them the only thing in your life. Have other things going for you at the same time. Think of the personals as an OK adjunct to other approaches, not as a substitute for going out and meeting people directly. Make the personals part of your network, as you saturate the field, increasing your chances by widening your exposure. Treat the personals like Saturday morning at the flea market. It's not the only place to shop, but you might very well pick up a bargain.

The Bars

There are probably more myths about gay bars than anything else in gay life other than gay partnerships. A patient of mine once put it this way: a gay bar would be the ideal place to meet someone, so that you would never have to go back there again. But if you can never meet someone in gay bars, you do have to go back there again, and again, to try to meet someone. I have heard from many of my patients, as well as from friends and acquaintances, that you cannot meet anyone in gay bars because they are full of shy people who never make their move, and stand-and-stare people who just go there to pose, preen, and reject.

In fact, gay bars are not the inherently bad places these and other cultural myths would have you believe. The problem is that gay men think, "I'll go to bars because I have no better place to go," then act in unproductive ways once they get there because they have convinced themselves that they are participating in nothing and that all is already lost. Their negativity in turn makes the bar experience negative. Particularly counterproductive is the, "Veni, Vidi, Victimized" approach to life, where you convince yourself you will be rejected, think the first person you speak to is, as expected, rejecting you, and recoil in anticipation of a turn-down, thereby proving your own point.

It is a fact that more connections are made in gay bars than people generally realize. Cynics just forget to count the ones that start small—with the introductions that everyone agrees do take place in bars, and on a regular basis.

I personally know many gay men who met their lovers in bars—many times removed. They just don't realize it because it took years to work their way through a flow chart of connections to reach their goal. In one case, here's how it happened: Matt met Ken, who introduced him to Gene, whose lover was Bob, who introduced him to Karl, who introduced him to Robert, who became his lover of a lifetime. Marlon also found his lover in a bar, a few steps removed. He found him through another man he knew, who introduced him to a friend, who invited him over for dinner, who had a guest staying overnight, who became Marlon's lover.

In assessing the outcome of bar cruising, gay men forget all about such productive linkages. Instead, they best remember the times they looked and no one looked back, or talked to someone and were met with stony silence. They forget that technically men like Marlon still met their lovers in a bar even though it didn't exactly happen overnight. In Marlon's case, that particular sequence took six years.

Instead of automatically speaking out against bars, what you need to do is make bars work for you. Here is how to make the bar experience productive. As a general principle, recognize that on the streets, in bars, the personals, or anywhere else, essentially the same rules apply, and that following them will create success for you wherever you are.

Be Active

It's not where you go, but what you do when you get there. Strike a balance between being too active and too passive, that is neither a wallflower nor a bulldozer be. Develop a friendly, interested, and available look and posture somewhere between a slouch and a pounce.

Plan Your Moves

Decide before you go what you plan to wear, and how you plan to talk and act, and with whom, when you get there. Some gay men make sure their appearance is appropriate for their circumstances. They ask themselves, "Will I hit a bar in a hotel, an elegant establishment, a local hangout, a muscle bar, or a leather bar?"

then dress accordingly. They refuse to wear leather to an A-gay bar, or a Persian lamb hat to the Ramrod. Others dress the way they want to wherever they are. I once knew a handsome Scandinavian who deliberately defied the cultural norms of the place he was in just so he could get the antiestablishment vote. Some thought he was not outstanding, just standing out. But it worked for him. I thought it was cute. So did the man he met who subsequently became his lover.

Be Task-Oriented

Before you get to the bars, decide if you are going there to have a good or a productive time. Don't go to have a good time then bitch that it isn't productive, or the reverse. Decide if you are there to drink, hear the music, or meet people, then act accordingly. If you are there to hear the music and move to the rhythm of the disco beat, you may need a better stereo system. If you are there to meet someone, check your anxiety at the door, and remember why you came in the first place. You have to do more than just say, "Ooh, being gay is so hard," when what you should be saying is, "Ooh, being out of step is so unproductive."

Do Not Undercut Your Own Purposes

Don't blame the bar if you cannot meet people there. Don't blame yourself either. Consider the possibility that your results are at least, in part, the predictable outcome of your actions.

Be Practical

You will probably never accomplish much if you enter a bar to gawk at the best-looking man in the place—admiring his tight blue jeans or other qualities that appeal to you sexually but not personally. You are not there to gratify your base instincts, you are there to make sensible choices and helpful tradeoffs. I don't want to hear, "Isn't he cute, can't you just see him bent over?" from you. What I want to hear is, "Isn't he great husband material, can't you just see him bent over a hot oven?" Now you already know from what has been said about successful gay

71

relationships that the two things are different, so why not start acting on what you already know, and do it tonight?

Be Flexible

Maybe he isn't your type, but maybe you are not flexible enough about type. Include in your calculations whether or not he is a particularly good type of his type, and how long it has been since you last found someone great of your type. Besides, someone who isn't your type can change, and if he cannot he probably knows a someone who is your type. You might even consider taking a lesson from the value investor in the stock market and putting your money on the Dogs of the Dow, realizing that a little sheep dip can make one of last year's underperformers into next year's little lamb.

Be Less Exotic in Your Tastes and Sexual Preferences

Avoid terrible extreme paraphilias (perversions) like pedophilia and sadism if, for no other reason (and there certainly are others), than that these limit the field of possible candidates. For example, many gay men say they could never fall in love with someone from the whips-and-chains set. A good general principle is that learning to love meat-and-potatoes sex may mean you will have fewer places to dine, but many more places to eat.

Be Less Critical of Others

As you avoid being perfectionistic and grandiose, going only for the top guy in the bar, master your negative attitudes toward people you deem flawed. For example, many gay men think someone else is "too old" for them. Thinking they know their own exact life expectancy, they avoid someone who might die before them, and thinking they know how they are going to hold up and exactly when they plan to fade, they try to avoid someone who might fade first (or who, in their book, has faded already). Here are your choices, put facetiously to make a point: younger than you—robbing the cradle; same age as you—narcissistic object choice; older than you—you must be a hustler. Put less facetiously, age doesn't matter and age differences don't count for as much as you might think. They matter the most to others who are out to dish you, which is often those who envy you and anything good you get. There are advantages and disadvantages to every arrangement, except the one between them dishing you and you being home plate.

Counter any exclusionary attitudes you might have about looks by asking yourself, "Why does he have to be good-looking?" Are you trying to impress your friends, or even your parents? Are you competing with the rest of the world and touting him as your Oscar? Are you putting too much emphasis on the sexual side of things?

Be Sensible

For one thing, be patient. Don't expect a direct response to your stimulus. Finding someone can take days, or even years, to work. Don't stop too soon. There are often many intermediate steps between first contact and final outcome. These can be slow but worth the effort. For another thing, be persistent. Keep on keeping on. Also be rational. Do, but don't overdo, bars. Staying out late is okay on weekends, but not during the week because you have to get up to go to work the next morning.

Take Care in Deciding Whom You Are Going to Approach

Pay attention to your self-protective instincts. If, for example, your feelings tell you to stay away from someone to spare yourself pain or danger, follow your impulses, at least for tonight, and hope that he is a regular and that you will get another chance to try again after sleeping on it.

Make Reasonable Choices while Still Aiming High

Avoid letting a low self-esteem make your choices for you, as in "He is too good for me, I don't have what it takes to get him." Don't avoid someone just because you think he will turn you down. That is just another way to sell yourself short due to fear. Many successful matches have been made between unequals in looks, intelligence, schooling, and wealth, partly because some gay men don't like, and won't pick, others who are too similar to them.

Determine who is going to make a good match for you too. Ask yourself not only who is going to accept you, but also whom you are going to accept.

Follow Through

Keep at a relationship for a while before giving up on it. I know someone who talks often about his difficulties with meeting people, and he always says the same thing: "No one I meet ever calls me back." When I ask him why he doesn't call them back he says, "Too pushy," "He rejected me by not calling me back and he isn't going to do that again," or, "He lives in the next town, just too inconvenient." So often finding a lover is not the issue. It is doing the right thing with the one you already found.

I know many gay men who won't see a new acquaintance from last night tonight, or ever again. There are many reasons why, most of which involve having guilty second thoughts about sex—yes, due to self-homophobia, the kind that plagues gay men almost more than homophobia from others. I discuss self-homophobia in greater depth in chapters 9 and 11. Right now, all you need to know is that persistence that gets you beyond the hump of morning-after remorse can lead to a relationship you will be glad finally happened.

Network

Bars might be bad places to find someone to go home with that very night, but they are good places to at least start heading in the right direction. Networking is just a form of taking the long way around to get where you are going safely, productively, and in one piece. You are taking a detour when the main route is completely blocked, or is not easily navigable.

You are also building a base. Meet a number of people and develop a large circle of friends. A good idea is to come to a bar with one friend, who will then introduce you to his friends. However you do it, make all the friends you can make and be nice to them all. They are (1) particularly important in your life when you don't have a lover, and (2) your means to finding a lover.

Networking can seem to take forever, but getting crazy, bypassing this important step, and trying to head right for your goal in a panic can, like most things done in a panic, lead to failure. To network effectively, you have to get over the feeling that just because you didn't meet a lover Saturday night, the night, and your life, was wasted. First, almost anything you do that is potentially productive, even if it doesn't help you achieve your goals immediately, is a good try, and good practice, not a waste of time. Second, by chance alone, some Saturdays will always be better than others. Third, it is always possible that you caught someone's eye and inserted yourself into his mind for future consideration.

When you feel impatient, try to remember that love stories usually take three hundred pages to unfold, and typically move forward only in the face of obstacles. In a way, be happy you didn't meet him tonight. Only in tragedies do people meet and marry on page one, and it's all downhill after that.

Be Nice

It is impossible to network effectively if you do things to insult and otherwise harm potentially important people in your network. Do not talk negatively behind someone's back or react to every less-than-stellar move they make, even if a provocation, with an equally less than stellar countermove, like a retaliation.

Be Careful

Pickups are the fastest way not to The Pines, but to Pine Lawn Cemetery. Avoid picking someone up and taking him home the same night. Get his phone number, give him a call, and get to know him first. They put that doorman there to protect you, what's the sense in dragging someone right by him to your death? The worst experience Frank had was on an occasion in which he took someone home. The man gave him a Mickey Finn and stole his credit cards, coin collection, and his dead lover's signet ring—the one he didn't want him buried in because he was afraid the undertaker would take it.

Having successfully navigated Step Five, you have learned that there are literally hundreds of places to go to meet a man and that eliminating possibilities just reduces your chances of finding someone for yourself. You have learned that the place is important and so is what you bring to it—in the form of motivation to succeed and goal-oriented activity, things that are just as important in a bar as anywhere else in life. Also important are patience and persistence that give your plans enough time to work, for even the best places take a while to provide. Don't count on any one place doing the trick for you. Wide regular exposure with an active posture and an accepting frame of mind is the order of the day, and has ultimately provided the wonderful things most men want to most of the gay men I treated and knew personally.

Now that you know where to go, you are ready to take Step Six and be as great as you can be when you get there.

6

Step Six: Look Great for Mr. Wonderful

Curiously, the very same gay men who overvalue others' looks may undervalue and neglect improving on their own, creating dating liabilities due to poor grooming or dress. Step Six is about overcoming these liabilities. Here are some ways you can improve how you look, if that is what you need to do, and some specific suggestions for enhancing the way you present yourself so that you can better appeal to his *six* senses: sight, smell, taste, hearing, touch, and *common*. Improving your appearance increases your choices and enhances your chances. You become less of a specialty item, not too eccentric, or too weird, to appeal to the masses—where by definition most of the opportunities lie.

However, improving your appearance may not be as easy as you think. Sometimes, changing how you look requires getting ahold of yourself and doing things that at first go against your grain. For example, some gay men dress to kill—their relationships that is. They do that because they have emotional obstacles to loving. They are like a straight woman I once treated. She said she wanted to find a husband and get married, yet she wore pointy black hats and a cape that made her look like a witch—with all the Totos in the neighborhood cringing in fear as she passed by. I finally persuaded her to change her outfit, but it wasn't easy. Fearing the consequences of getting close, she actually hesitated to look seductive and was deliberately trying to scare men off.

First, I ask you to collect as many opinions about how you look and behave as you possibly can. Find out if others are dissing you, and not because they envy you either. Ask people, "Am I neglecting my appearance? Am I neglecting my clothes? Is there anything I might be saying or doing that is off-putting, or bizarre?" After you ask how you're doing, listen to the answer. Ask your advisers several times. Usually, the first response is flattery, until they sense that you really want to know. Then they might even tell you the truth.

Your best bet for an advisor is that truly honest, truly bitchy, friend or "sister" who aggravates your paranoia by telling you what you don't want to hear but need to know. He or she covers all the appearance problems you have, outlines the kinds of judgments that other gay men may make about how you look and behave, and suggests specific remedies. Don't get angry with your poor critical "sister." Take his criticism seriously and make what changes are indicated.

If you accidentally find out what bad things people are saying about you, use what you hear to improve yourself. Turn things around on them by paying attention and taking their comments to heart. It's called living better as your best revenge.

Ignore the opinions of flatterers who say only nice things about you; dummies who aren't smart enough to spot your flaws; narcissists who don't care about you because they don't even know you exist; and competitives who would just love to see you look bad so that they can look better.

Here are some specifics.

Take good care of yourself physically. Good looks and good health go hand in hand, so drink less, or not at all; don't smoke; and only take medications that are prescribed by a *knowledgeable* physician. Eat well. Give up junk food because of its deleterious effects on your body and health and because other people watching you eat it get a negative message. Health fiends send the message: "I am actively keeping up my appearance." Now others think, "Maybe his collagen will collapse after forty years, but at least he will still have the strength, courage, and desire to catch it when it falls."

If you are up to it physically, you, like most gay men, and especially those beyond a certain age, can likely use a gym makeover. In the gym, you tone your body, build some muscles (in moderation), and lose what fat and weight you can, while getting to know the man on the next machine. Walk for a half an hour or more each day—another way to go where He might be. Staying physically healthy means having regular physicals, too.

Fix your back as well as your front. Remember the times your barber held up a mirror to the back of your head so that you could see what was going on there? This was more than a good way to check on your haircut. It was also a paradigm for a good way for you to improve your life.

Remember that there are two sides to you. Living as we do in the land of the bad haircut, where the barber is also the mayor, and, worse, vice versa, I have become sensitive to how few men, straight and gay alike, pay attention to the backs of their heads (and bodies), and how it often shows most in their haircuts. They have no real idea what's going on back there. But others do because they see them going as well as coming. Don't go to the country barber instead of the city hairstylist just to save a couple of bucks. Some local men do unspeakable things around the ears, leaving them to protrude unnecessarily, and to the nape of the neck, making that potentially gay sexy curve into a perfectly dreadful, perfectly straight line. Of course, leaving your hair unkempt, uncombed, uncut, and unwashed is taking an even bigger risk.

Pay special attention to your skin and complexion. Cure any skin ailment you might have, and get it soon before it leaves permanent scars. Remove troublesome and ugly warts and moles, don't smoke so that you don't develop gray skin and wrinkles before you are very old, and wear shoes that are kind to your feet without leaving unsightly corns and bunions behind.

Be attentive to your bodily hygiene. Especially if you smoke, keep your mouth and teeth clean and fresh. Keep your teeth white by brushing frequently and having them bleached if your dentist feels that could help. Always floss or use a water pic before a night out so that you don't smile with a piece of something on your front teeth. Ask others about possible bad breath and treat that seriously. It just might mean you have a medical problem that needs caring for.

Keep your fingernails short and clean, and shave, grow a beard, or have a neat in-between, semi-long shave, but avoid stubble. Use deodorant freely. Bathe regularly, and, considering how many gay men are foot fetishists, pay particular attention to your feet, which you should wash as carefully as you wash the rest of you. Keep your toenails clipped, and clean under these nails too. Whenever possible, cure toenail (and foot) fungus before it ruins the nails permanently.

Be especially on guard in the beginning of relationships when people don't know you well enough for their positive feelings about you to have fully developed. Finally, don't wear cheap perfume, or any perfume at all. I know of several cases where someone didn't like the toilet water and with it threw out the baby.

Make style important. A good rule is to neither a stereotype nor a satire on yourself be. Look hard at those men whose appearance grabs you, and imitate them slavishly—down to the shoes, socks, and backpack they carry.

Many of my patients were successful precisely because they followed a middle-of-the-road style of dress, the one prevailing at a given time in more conservative, A-gay circles. They knew that extraordinary appearances reduce the pool of available candidates and possible admirers. Makeup, dark suntans, and tattoos are specialty items that don't appeal to everyone. Certain looks, like blond hair with dark roots, or blond hair topping off a beard dyed black, can get you branded as an eccentric, and Mr. Right will go on to the next person.

Of course, to an extent, what you wear depends on who and where you are, where you are coming from or going to later, and the season of the year. But mostly, simple jeans and intact, nicely-fitting T-shirts and a cool coat from the sporting-goods store appeal to everybody, while platform shoes, tight spandex pants, or torn T-shirts or jeans are probably not going to attract that successful stockbroker of your dreams. Limit your jewelry to a tasteful ring, and perhaps a cross or star on a chain around your neck. Duck's ass haircuts, turtleneck shirts under sweaters or jackets, T-shirts showing out from under regular shirts or, double ecch, from under polo shirts, a sweatshirt that says "porno star" on it, and long mink coats accompanying charm bracelets and nine large rings on four fingers are, at least in certain important circles, *de rigueur mortis*. Being creative or original, attempting to express something unique about yourself, or even creating a new style for others to follow is OK, but bachelorhood is not time to be eccentric. Remember that one bad item can spoil the whole bunch. It doesn't take much to "look like a tourist," so be very careful here. Any deviation makes you stand out, like someone on New York's Fifth Avenue with a pair of Bermuda shorts, a map, and a camera, giving as well as getting the picture.

Your underwear is doubly important in case (1) you get unlucky and get into a car accident, or (2) get lucky. As you plan what underwear to wear, remember that if you have gotten this far, now is no time for a practical joke in the form of little logos on the fabric or snakes coming out of the fly (or a ring on something other than your fingers and toes).

Your glasses should always be in style, not dated. After all, like underwear, they serve a dual purpose. They help you see what you are getting, and they help him see the good thing he is getting into.

Drag is a clown's costume. People are entertained, but they go home after the performance. At least be consistent. If you wear drag, be sure to also wear a lampshade on your head, and a bra over, not under, your shirt (or blouse).

Some of my patients expressed their emotional disturbances in their style of dress. While the following styles are OK in certain circles, they may not be for you:

- The just emerged from the shower, long stringy hair and everything else resolutely natural too, look
- The wild man of Borneo and/or the dirt-bag (schmutzophrenia) look
- The flaming look
- The space-cadet, interplanetary look
- The lounge-lizard, leisure-suit, con-man look
- The shy, prissy, retiring look
- The schlemiel look
- The shoddy, sale items from remainder stores saved-a-buck-spoiled-the-child look

- The retro, behind-the-times, look
- The leather and chains (sadomasochistic) look
- The ring-through-the-nose-eyebrow-tongue-lip, how-is-anyone-going-to-do-it-with-me-anyway rebellious look

These looks were not due to simple bad grooming that resulted from carelessness. They were more than the sloppy man's knots in his shoelaces that signaled laziness or lack of concern about appearance. They were distancing behaviors, however unconsciously motivated.

If you have one of these looks, make sure that this is a look you really like, and that it is a positive endeavor to look your very best and not a way to say some very negative things about yourself, or to tell others to go away.

There is a problem called body dysmorphic disorder where you focus on a nonexistent or minor problem with your appearance, like a spot on your nose or a slight facial asymmetry, to the extent that you are consumed by it, and will even check over and over in any available reflecting surface, like car bumpers, to see if it's still there and determine how bad it is. People with this disorder will sometimes go to extremes to make repairs that make the problem worse rather than better. This goes deeper than just an appearance problem, and requires professional assistance.

Avoid broadcasting your deep anxieties in body language. Try not to slump as you walk as if you are depressed, convey feelings of anxiety by nail biting or hair twirling, or manifest distancing behaviors by neck craning to see everyone that walks in the room when you should instead be looking at Him. I was watching an older man eating dinner all by himself in a semi-gay restaurant. He wouldn't have been bad looking if: his posture were better; his beard were trimmed; his clothes weren't all dark dirty brown; he didn't let his face hang down into his soup, depressed style; and he canned that newspaper he was reading and looked up and around occasionally to indicate that he was available.

Avoid manneristic movements in public. Once, I saw a gay man sticking his tongue into his cheek, making a dimple, and pushing the protuberance back with his finger, then repeating the same thing somewhere else in his mouth to tighten his facial muscles. Try not to make a nonverbal statement about your special fantasy of what it means to be gay. Instead, try to make a nonverbal statement about being good husband material. Mugging, swishing, or any other behavior that gets you attention and laughs instead of admiration and love detracts from the quiet refinement that makes an eligible man think he can introduce you to his mother without having to make excuses for his choice, and without making the mother feel that she is not losing a son, but gaining a rival.

Of course, the specific look you choose depends in part on who you want to look at you, and what specifically you are trying to accomplish with him. Intuit, mind read, and be that good judge of character to infer the effect you are having on a specific him. Gear your dress to what Mr. Wonderful wants you to wear. Play to his fetish. For example, with underwear think of what he, not you, might like. For you, underwear is for warmth, comfort, and protection, but for him it's fashionable or sexy. Does the kind of man you are interested in like Wall Street types who wear boxers, or athletic types who wear Jockey shorts? Don't walk around in construction boots with a potential lover who likes Wall Street types. When indicated, change for him tonight, or at least promise to change for him tomorrow. Does he seem to be staring bullets at your spit curls? Maybe he thinks they are fetching, but maybe he doesn't like them, and if you suspect that that is the case head for the men's room and comb them out. Dressing creatively is what you do for you while imagining you are doing it for him. You have two concerns: what you think looks good on you, and what others may think about how you look and how they respond to you.

Here is a good general rule I suggest that my patients follow. If you are trying to meet someone for a committed relationship, try to pass muster at the mall. Look a bit suburban, set off with just a touch of élan.

Age gracefully. People always know how old you are anyway, so trying to hide your age is futile. Face lifts make you look young from afar, but you want to get close. Besides, when you have a face lift you are selling your soul to the devil, who comes back and reclaims it by making your face lift collapse after seven or so years of good luck. As you get older, accept that you are balding or turning gray, and go bald neatly and turn gray honestly. Remember that growing more hair at the back and sides of your head doesn't make up for not having it in the front. Instead, the excess in one place just calls attention to the absence in another. Toupees and bad hair dye (especially jet black) fool nobody. Unstylish combovers and bad hair transplants, where people see not lawn but sod, are also unsatisfactory. Age-inappropriate props are out too. A common problem with a Porsche is that by the time you can afford one, it may not go with you at all. All these things exude an air of desperation that sends others the message that you feel defective the way you are. Acting like you don't like yourself prompts others to agree.

Recognize, too, that looking beautiful involves more than just superficial things like what clothes you wear, although these are very important. Looking beautiful outside involves being beautiful inside, which can mean playing to his fantasies, making your beauty in the eye of your beholder. Smiling instead of scowling at him is often enough to make him feel good enough about you to make you look good to him just as you are, no matter what you are wearing.

Finally, put all my advice in perspective. Even the most serious appearance problems don't hinder you that much. Others may not love you at first sight, but you will simply have to find ways to get past that, something you might not have to do if you are perfection itself. But after first impressions, you pull equal with everyone else. As always, for less than perfect specimens (and even for them), building a network of people is just as important, and usually just as effective, as trying to get someone to fall in love with you at first sight.

Doing some of the things I recommend takes money, and many people are unable to follow my suggestions because they are on a tight budget. Having money is especially necessary when it comes to keeping up your dental and physical health. If money is short, and finding someone is more important to you than free time, consider taking an extra job to pay the bills. Besides, you might stand a better chance of meeting someone on a second job than anywhere else. At the very least, if you have a second job you will impress anyone you do meet with your ambition and seriousness of purpose. Also, you will be more or less forced not to dissipate. That alone can keep you a healthy, sane, and valuable commodity in what can sometimes at least seem to be a very frustrating buyer's market.

Having climbed Step Six, you now look your best for him. But that's not enough. You also have to put your best foot forward and act your best too. To find Mr. Right, it always helps to be Mr. Wonderful yourself. Step Seven shows you how you can make yourself so pleasing to him that he will find you, just because he finds you irresistible.

7

Step Seven: Be Great for Mr. Wonderful

Relationships are like baseball. People do their best pitching to people who can catch. That's why before you can find Mr. Right, you have to be Mr. Right, and that's what Step Seven is about. When you ask, "What are the qualities I seek in Mr. Right?" also ask, "What will make me Mr. Right for him?" When you ask, "What do I see in him?" also ask, "What does he see in me?" Positive personal characteristics can increase your chances of connecting in a number of ways: first, they contribute directly to your appeal to strangers, or relative strangers, those new people you meet who size you up rather quickly during the first moments of an encounter—the time when gay men make snap and sometimes lasting judgments about you, as you make about them. You will be revealing yourself, willingly or no, so you should have a desirable self to reveal. While a few of the qualities I list in this chapter take a while to become obvious to someone who doesn't know you, gay men usually have their antennae out, and are experts at inferring. This makes your qualities obvious right from the start, and they play a major role in what, if anything, happens next.

They also make for good luck, which is more attitudinal than you might think, depending as it does on such factors as persistence and sincerity. They make for good tactics too, for these are highly dependent on traits such as warmth and empathy, and on developing a good reputation in the miniworld within which you are looking, one that is indispensable to getting the "referrals" you need to find what you are looking for.

Insightful self-observations about your character form one basis for useful corrective actions you can take to improve an image derailed by any temporary lapses in judgment. You can also enhance your positive personal qualities by picking good people to identify with. Far too many gay men identify with movie stars, but do not look at the fact that many movie stars have been divorced over and over again. My suggestion is to forget about Joan, Judy, Bette, and Elizabeth, and pick as an identification model someone substantial in the community.

Here are some good positive personal characteristics to have if you are looking to find a lifetime partner. They make you everybody's type. The more of them you have, the better your chances of finding someone, having him accept you, and making a go of the relationship.

Some of the traits that I consider positive others consider negative. For example, I consider passivity associated with a willingness to surrender, compromise, and adapt to be a positive personality feature. Others might consider it a sign not of strength but of weakness. Work with what is comfortable for you.

Many of these traits are good for everybody to have—gay men, straight men and women, lesbians, and bisexuals. Others are especially helpful for gay men to have. For example, considering how two men, gay or straight, often compete with each other, the ability to accommodate is an especially important personal attribute for gay men looking for a stable, committed relationship.

The following list of traits will also serve as an outline of good traits you might be looking for in a partner. Together with the traits that go into making up Mr. Right presented in Step Four, they offer a rounded picture of the happy interlocking qualities that make up a successful couple.

The Ability to Accommodate

Being accommodating doesn't mean being a wimp, abdicating your personal identity or independence, becoming a slave, or allowing yourself to be abused just for the sake of a relationship. It doesn't mean saying, "I don't mind," when others do things that upset you badly, and it doesn't mean letting negative feelings about and actions toward you go on indefinitely without attempting to resolve, or without just calling a halt to, them. The goal of being an accommodating gay man means developing certain skill.

Don't Sweat the Small Stuff

That means getting less upset about minor matters, which allows you to be forbearing while you get to know other people and give them the test of time. Besides, I strongly believe that small stuff goes away when people get involved in a relationship where they feel wanted and loved. I've seen things like bitchiness disappear completely in the context of a loving relationship. Just imagine if you dumped him because he was a bitch, when you could have made him less bitchy just by hanging on to him.

Be Cooperative

In my personal experience, the gay men most successful at finding and keeping relationships are those who are agreeable, up to a point. Instead of insisting, "I am me, take it or leave it," and, "If you don't like me the way I am, well too bad," you quickly learn what he likes and wants, and, whenever possible, give it to him. Try to eliminate the word "no" from your mind and vocabulary when you are looking for a partner. The ability to pick up clues about what he likes and wants immediately and correctly can prove especially useful during the first few moments of an encounter. That is decision time, when a wrong move can make you an instant loser. For example, we have all asked someone we just met, "What do you do for a living?" just to make conversation. We are nervous, don't quite know what to say, and are fishing for where to go next. But there is no next if the person we ask gets up on his high horse and, instead of excusing our nervousness, rejects us by enforcing some basic rule he imagines is good to have, like, "I make it a practice never to tell anyone what I do until I know him better because I don't want to be judged by my profession," or makes a cute (hasty) remark like, "Do you mean professionally or in bed?" If this is you, think twice about that response, and consider just answering the question. Don't allow him to talk you into anything dangerous, like getting into his car before you get to know him. However, after you have determined he is safe, humor him, and go where he wants to go, like to a new bar he might want to try tonight, or home early instead of waiting for last call.

Robin, a personal friend, asked Fred to leave the bar early so that he could go to bed at a reasonable hour. As a writer, Robin liked to get up and start working very early in the morning—around 5:00 A.M.—and was right from the start looking for someone to go along with his schedule, not someone who wanted to stay up until 12:00 A.M. on a weeknight and then sleep late the next day. Fred said, "Yes." Robin said, "Yes!"

Keeping your schedule flexible is another good idea. Should he ask you, "Are you free tomorrow night?" don't answer, "No, and not only that (listing all your previous engagements in numbing detail), this is a bad month for me." The preferred reply is, "Yes," then if you are really busy, make a few phone calls and make room for him on your schedule, even if that means juggling that schedule to fit him in. Alternatively, try a counter offer, "No, but would you be free the next night?" Keep going back and forth until you've made a date. You'll both feel good, and have something to look forward to.

Recently, a patient of mine, a New York man in his fifties with plenty of money and free time, said about a potential partner, someone he could easily have fallen in love with, "Not him, he lives in Connecticut." He called him "geographically undesirable" as an excuse for not pursuing him. Instead, he should have adapted and found a way to go where this man lived. Here is a place where a disco philosophy might have come in handy. As the song more or less goes: "Get on that love train."

Avoid Competitive Struggles

Your new friend brags, "I am in town for an important business conference." Don't reply, either, "Boy I wish I had a mission in life, too," or "You think your mission in life is important, just listen to mine." Simply say, "How nice," and add your version of, "Sounds like if we get something going together we can afford a Jaguar." Don't select a loser just to be sure that he doesn't show you up, and don't pick a winner and try to turn him into a loser just so that you can show him up. Sometimes it's even best to play up your own weaknesses, at least for now. If you sense he's one of those men who feel better about themselves when they think they have more than you do, instead of coming on strong, play down your strengths, and let him have the spotlight. You don't actually have to act or be inferior to a competitive man like this, but it is a mistake to brag to such a man about all the librettos you can quote word for word and in the original Italian too, and how just yesterday your publisher asked you to complete Puccini's *Turandot* for him. It is much better to keep your major assets under wraps, and save your brilliance for later, when it might be less blinding.

Be Reliable

Make sure others know what they can count on with you. If you make a date for next time, keep it and be prompt. Don't call up to cancel or to say you are just leaving when you are supposed to be arriving. Don't arrive half an hour late, then say, tepidly, "The time just got away from me," or, "I didn't bother to call because I thought you would already know that it was slow going in the snow." While waiting for a table outside a favorite restaurant in Chelsea, I often see men waiting for their dates, or lovers, who are late to show. They are really upset, annoyed, and even in actual pain as the minutes go by. It is horrifying to watch them pace. Then when the other person finally shows up, they make light of the delay, as if his finally arriving makes everything OK. One says, "I'm sorry," and the other says, "That's all right." But while the first one thinks, "Since he said it is OK I am home safe and can do it again," the second one thinks, "I never want to go through that one more time," and looks for someone new.

Don't Be a Social Outcast Just to Be Chic

Accommodating gay men do not act disaffected, learning what society thinks is right just so that they can do the opposite. They do not believe that being different is the greatest thing about being gay, then express this freedom symbolically by wearing platform shoes, spit curls, studded belts, scanty tank tops that reveal ghastly tattoos, tight clothes that reveal semi-private parts, or jeans with tears in the knees they put in themselves to be stylish. They also don't carry backpacks to the opera or opera glasses to the Outback. They plan to die old, rich, and married, not young, broke, and alone—the latter just so that they can be one of the crowd that likes to spite and defeat authority—an attitude that however mature it might look is still left over from when your parents tried to toilet train you and you decided you had a much better idea.

Be Flexible about Type

As an accommodating gay man, you have broad tastes in men. Many different types of men are potentially right for you. Distinguish reasonable exclusion criteria (what you absolutely don't want in a man) from rigidity that leads you to keep good things out of your life, as in, "I just hate dependent men," "I don't like older men," or "Scratch him, he's a member of the bridge-and-tunnel set."

Have to have a hairy man? Is that really what you want, or are you just trying to be masculine by osmosis because you fear being a sissy? I had one patient who only wanted hairy men, and in the meantime discarded dozens of great hairless ones. He had spent hours and hours as a child bemoaning the fact that his own chest wasn't hairy, and that meant that he was not a "real boy." In treatment he reformed, and instead of picking someone who knew how to grow hair, he picked someone who knew how to grow to love him.

Accept Less Than 100 Percent in a Man

Give up the search for the picture-perfect lover. Humans have flaws and all relationships are missing something, often because it is still too early for it to have developed. Keep your expectations reasonable—high enough so that you can be satisfied, and low enough so that you can be successful. Fixed immutable types and standards should yield to second choices, and you might even be willing to accept others' rejects. (Eager, actually—for of the two, the "rejectee" is often the better choice than the "rejector," for, after all, it's always the nice guys that, at least in the beginning, really do finish last.)

William and Mark, two personal friends, both had a healthy attitude about their respective preferences. When they first met, William wasn't crazy about Mark—he wasn't a prize catch for Mark because he wasn't hairy enough, his skin was pink and not swarthy, his shoes were as sensible as he was, and he personally didn't like or need the rescuing tricks William loved to perform. In his turn, Mark wasn't crazy about William because Mark was out to find someone really cute he could show off at the disco (the very disco where recently during Tea-dance a bouncer tried to spirit off the cute man he brought with him). And here was William, so ordinary look-ing that Mark could easily get him through the front door, past the bouncer, with-out so much as creating a stir. But each rethought what they wanted in a man, recognized that sometimes relationships are a collection of vices that add up to a virtue, and decided they liked each other enough to give things a chance.

It doesn't help to perversely get interested in someone just because you sense that he is difficult or impossible to have. Don't be that sort of person who only likes challenges, someone who, like a rabbit hunter, is mainly attracted to what runs away when chased.

Instead, make a list of people in ascending order of preference and, recogniz-ing how often your powers of discrimination fail, give the ones near the bottom of your list a try. Create lovers out of people with potential. At least don't pass over a good possibility, someone who might not have had what it took in the beginning, but could have been made over into someone just right for you. Maybe you overlooked him because he wasn't dressed right, or you relied on some other first impression to judge him. Could he have been a gift to you that you were too busy, too preoccupied, or even too stuck up to unwrap? A good trick I sometimes recommend to my patients is to spot a couple where one man is obviously better-looking than the other, determine if they are committed to each other or just friends, decide if you are willing to take the risks associated with moving in on a couple, then, if you decide you are and think that they are just friends, go after the one who is less good-looking. The handsome one, if he is any sort of person, will be delighted that someone is finally showing interest in his "sister," and the one who is less good-looking will be delighted that someone is showing interest in him, for him an experience that is distinctly out of the ordinary.

Squelch Extraordinary Sexual Appetites

Perhaps more than anything else, a desire for exotic sex limits the field of possible candidates. In contrast, accepting and learning to love "meat and potatoes" gay sex means you will be busier than if you demand only gourmet foods. You may look down on McDonald's, but it's always full. At the very least, don't act wild from the start, suggesting pornography or sex toys.

Don't Resist the Urge to Merge

If it is what he wants, go for a merger relationship—that kind of relationship where when two people fall in love it is completely, and when two people mate they are inseparable for a day, never mind for life. While psychologists generally frown on mergers, I feel that mergers are great for some people. They give you something to be involved in when you are not having sex.

Soft-Pedal Your Identity

Don't be a strong personality right from the start, especially should you sense that there are personality conflicts between the two of you. Recognize that few men say at the beginning, "I love you; stay just the way you are." Self-expression is important and you should try to write the play of life the way you feel it. But the best writers always keep their audience in mind, and when it comes to wedding ceremonies, "I do," always beats "I am."

Self-Confidence

Self-confident gay men are OK with themselves. They have a reasonable amount of self-esteem. They don't feel too small, and their ego isn't too big.

If they feel undesirable, they try to hide it just as they might try to hide any other personal problem they might have. To avoid handing a new man an exclusion criterion on a plate, at first self-confident men only admit to having those problems others must know about right from the start, such as a positive HIV status.

Self-confident gay men are resourceful too. As one, you find ways to compensate for your shortcomings. You compensate for less-than-perfect beauty by dressing neatly and attractively. You find a way to make being short cute; gangly imposing; fat motherly; and skinny wiry.

Self-confident gay men promote themselves too. As I studied the lives of gay men who are still alone, I discovered that one thing they had in common was that they were bad salespeople who didn't advertise themselves properly, or at all. For one thing, they failed to make their availability known, because they were, and acted, ashamed of who they were, and of what they wanted. They neglected to tell everyone, "I am looking for a lover and want to settle down and get married." They wanted to avoid being accused of self-promotion, or criticized for being stuck on themselves, or condemned for being too serious about life. But others couldn't find them because they didn't know where they were, or that they were looking.

Never expect other people to guess correctly what you are thinking and really want. Gay men seem to read minds, but not always accurately or completely. Coyly, some gay men say, "I don't want a lover," and expect others to know, "He's just saying that—down deep he really does want one." You may be unpleasantly surprised if you expect others to see through you and tear down an impenetrable façade.

Some things related to self-confidence are difficult to fake convincingly, but it's worth a try. For example, I know many gay men no one seemed to be interested in—until they were in a committed relationship. Then everyone pursued them. Was it because everybody wanted a man who was already taken? I don't think so, or at least that was only part of it. I think it was because in being desired, they felt desirable, and that showed. They looked sexy and became irresistible because they were happy, and they were happy because they were involved in a relationship that worked.

What you don't do can be as important as what you do. Never put yourself down. Certainly never criticize yourself in public. Complainers are not gainers either. People are willing to care for a lover if he gets sick after years of being together; but they are rarely willing to take on a person who needs not a lover but a nurse, right from the start. Professionally, I hesitate to take on a patient who calls me up and asks straight out if I prescribe valium. But if I have a patient already in therapy who needs valium, they are welcome to it. So don't tell someone you just met how lonely and needy you are. Be that stable, relatively independent person who reassures new acquaintances that you will carry your own weight in a relationship. That means when he asks you, "What kind of work do you do?" you have a good, truthful answer you can give him without blushing, lying, or making excuses for being unemployed, and when he asks you, "Where do you live?" you have a real address and phone number to give him—someplace he can reach you should he want to call you back. He wants a ball. Don't give him a chain.

Self-confident gay men are also active without being aggressive. As a self-confident gay man, you take the initiative in dating and make it clear you want him without pushing yourself to the point of making yourself unwelcome. People who send double messages often stay single.

Self-confident gay men are resilient too. You should handle rejection well, and don't give up too easily because you feel each little turndown reaffirms a personal unworthiness, or a perceived hopelessness of your existential predicament as a gay man.

However, being active and forthright doesn't mean being a desperada. A desperada, while working on something good, uses his eyes not for navigating, but for wandering, cruising someone, and at the same time looking the place over to see if there is something better out there, a kind of picture-in-picture scenario. A desperada looks as if he will take anything he can get. If you are a desperada, you project the wrong image as you jump from one person to another in a bar, or at a party, writing down your phone number for everyone, handing out your cards indiscriminately, asking everyone if they know that one, screaming "Isn't she cute?" and pushing too hard for introductions all around.

Motherliness

In my opinion, the quickest way to a man's heart is through his umbilical cord. Gay men don't want layers of pretense and defense, and they do want more than just sex. When they look for a lover, they want companionship, security, and gratification of their dependency needs. They want a mother, that is a nurturer, not one who worries about them or who rejects, controls, or castrates them. Remoteness, unsociability, or any other hint that you are a cold teat can be a turnoff, so be a warm one, giving lots of milk. Of course, I only mean for you to give milk symbolically. Offer to buy a man a drink or dinner. It makes the best opening line of them all. It is symbolic of being a friend, a caretaker, and a nurse. It will cost you, but not as much as all those overpriced drinks and dinners you will have to buy for yourself for the rest of your life if you never get married at all.

Warmth and Kindness

Hide your bitchiness. When it comes to sarcasm and other hostile attitudes, stingers protect the wasp—but they also provoke the bug spray. Be less critical. I am always amazed at those gay men who say they want a lover, then turn around and bitch all good possibilities out. Perhaps they equate being a bitch with having impeccable, aristocratic taste, or even with being macho. Once, I suggested that a friend paint his studio apartment white to make it look bigger. A bitch overheard me and, butting in, told him not to listen to me, because what did I know anyway, it actually made it look smaller. This man was undermining me and showing his competitiveness. He acted this way with everyone he met. He is still single, still competing, still looking, still not finding, and now he has even more to bitch about, in his little apartment with the colorful walls closing in on him.

Smiling at people is as good an idea as ideas get. When others smile at you, as they mostly will if you have a smile on your face, do not respond by thinking, "What did he mean by that—I don't know him." Instead, return the smile graciously. Just today I was admiring (not cruising) a gay man shlepping bags of groceries home from the supermarket in the West Village, thinking, "How sweet, how domestic." He looked back at me, smiled, and winked. What a great way to start a relationship, and what did it cost him?

Do not, however, respond to a seductive look with a seductive look back. Instead, respond with that smile and wink. Seductive looks back have a way of misfiring. It is particularly hard to distinguish between seductiveness, inscrutability, staring bullets, being a dullard, and being completely otherwise preoccupied.

Nice gays don't set people up either. You don't ask to be fed just so that you have a hand to bite. Indirect verbal and nonverbal insults are not in your vocabulary, and you avoid always putting yourself first while overlooking how others might feel. You may get angry, but at least you try to express your anger appropriately. You don't say or do anything really hurtful to, or about, someone else, remembering that anger is always a black mark against a relationship, and one that you might not be able to erase. Anything that even smacks of saying, "You are not personally or sexually attractive," can never really be taken back. Like a stain on the tie, often the best that can be done is to lighten it; but the telltale spot always remains.

Try to avoid making Freudian slips, like off-putting slips of the tongue. Don't be like my patient who told everyone to go away with a corrupted greeting on his answering machine: "This is John. I am unavailable."

An almost guaranteed method for successful networking is never to dish people. Even defend others someone else is dishing. If someone says, "That is a paranoid queen if ever I saw one," counter with, "That makes him a good detective, doesn't it?" Don't forget that people overhear the dishing you do (you want them to, don't you?) and that sometimes the negative response you get from Mr. Next is due to his reaction to what he overheard you saying to, or about, Mr. Last.

Be noncritical as you talk to him about others, and to others about him. Forget about insulting others. He will take your statements meant for someone else personally, thinking, "I'm next."

Take his side whenever possible. Avoid expressing differences of opinion right from the start. If he says, "What a dump," referring to the bar you are in, don't insist that it is great. If you cannot be completely supportive of him, then at least keep your lips firmly approximated.

Do keep your philosophy of life to yourself at first. Discussions of religion and politics during the first few minutes, or hours, of a relationship are not a particularly good idea. Brilliance can be disconcerting. Yes, the main theme from that popular new musical was stolen from an obscure thirteenth-century monody and the composer should be shot for being such an obvious thief. But such a discussion creates tension, and makes him feel uneasy, even if he might agree with you.

Do forgive him when your new man does something wrong and hurts you. If he snaps at you, reassure him with words and sentiments like, "You said what you felt, I don't mind, I will get over it." That way he gets something out of his system and the relationship gets a second chance. Do wait for any annoyances you might have with him to subside. In the meantime, say nothing instead of saying something that you can never take back, and instead of walking away to look for someone else. Back off and cool it; or take time out and get away, either to the bar to buy a drink, or to the men's room. You can try falling in love with people who give you a lot of crap at the beginning, knowing how often the crap stops when the loving starts. Don't, however, become a pushover. Do disabuse him gently of any wrong-headed ideas he might have about you. For example, if he insults you, try to rescue the day by asking him why, what he had in mind, or what is bothering him, and by giving him some reasons to reconsider.

One day at his favorite gay gym, Miles, a personal friend of mine, set his gym bag down on the bench. Stephen, a complete stranger, asked him, rather rudely, to move it because he wanted to sit down. Miles shot back, "Don't tell me what to do," and Stephen said, "And who are you, big shot?" Miles could have given Stephen a dirty look. Instead he called a halt to the negativity. He pulled back, smiled and said, "Kiss me and you'll find out." Both laughed, forgot about the gym bag, and made a date instead of a vendetta .

Withhold judgment of others until you get to know them well by filtering your first impressions through your second thoughts, to see if your first impressions were wrong. Consider the possibility that you don't know a sow's ear even when you see one, and that what you at first think is a sow's ear may in fact be a silk purse. After all, as you probably already know from experience, just because something is long and hairy and flicks when you touch it doesn't mean that it actually is a sow's ear.

Correct for defensiveness and anxiety. People start off defensive, but beneath that negative surface and all the mistakes and off days, what others call creeps can be your catch, and what others see as a molehill can be your mountain. I advise my patients to treat new acquaintances like they treat common objects on the craft shows. Make that ordinary oatmeal box into an extraordinary cachepot, just the sort of thing you might want around the house.

Do understand how anxious some people are when they first meet you—just as you are when you first meet them. Meeting new people makes people nervous and nerves make people inept because they feel vulnerable. During the first few minutes, both of you are experiencing a kind of performance anxiety. This is at its height in the first moments of a relationship the same way it is at its height in the first minutes of giving a speech. So wait until the awkwardness works its way out before you make major decisions about whether or not he is right for you. Respect his little quirks too. If he seems afraid of crowds, offer to try that new bar down the road that's empty because no one else besides the two of you wants to go there.

Try to see the good in new acquaintances. If he seems grandiose, perhaps it is just because he is grand. Once, in my bitchier days, I met a nice young fellow in an Upper East Side bar and asked him what he did for a living. He replied, "I am writing a musical." "Oh," I said, "What do you call it?" "I Feel Wonderful," was his answer. "Oh, but how will you feel when it flops?" I cleverly retorted. He sensibly removed himself from me. Years later, I found out that this very modest and friendly man went on to write a number of musicals, including a little play known as *Hello, Dolly!*

Try to bring out his best qualities by complimenting him for what he does right instead of criticizing him for what he does wrong. Being complimentary to him is often the simplest and best way to his heart. For one thing, it speaks to a need most people have to be seen as the most wonderful and the most important person in the world, and to prevail with you. Think of your new sow as all ears, just looking for someone to whisper something nice into them. That is what the behaviorists call positive feedback.

Always treat everyone well. Treat someone who comes over to say hello just as you might treat a guest you have invited into your home. If you don't like a particular person who is flirting with you, you can still be friendly without committing yourself to him. If you want to turn someone down, there are ways to do it without being cruel. "I appreciate the offer, but no thanks," will do, no explanation necessary. Don't make his interest in you an occasion to puff up your ego by rejecting him just to make yourself feel powerful and superior.

In conclusion, you are making relationships paramount. You are willingly losing a minor skirmish to be able to win a major war. If instead of being bitchy you are sweet and nice, others will find you attractive because they will see you through a warm haze that bypasses the reality of superficialities and evaluate you according to the rose-colored lens you have given them to view you with.

Focus

Focus on relationships. Work hard at finding and keeping them, without being coy and hesitant, inept, unmotivated, or distracted by alcohol, the buffet table, or the next passing beauty. Caution: being focused on, and single-minded about, finding a lover doesn't mean neglecting or hurting your family and friends in the process, because being nice to them:

- is good practice for being nice to everyone else, ultimately to that one special man in your life;
- gives you someone to fall back on in the hard times pretty much guaranteed to be there as you search;
- keeps up your referral sources, for even dull straight relatives might know someone sharp and gay for you; and
- avoids your getting a bad reputation that follows you around like cheap perfume.

Being patient goes along with being focused. As a patient gay man, don't assume that if you don't get something tonight then you will never get it. Be willing to wait. Don't push too hard, forcing and breaking things. Don't treat problems like a bottle with the lid stuck, banging it on the tabletop in frustration until it breaks. Frantic searching is a scattershot approach that leaves you angry and frustrated, without a specific destination in mind, and with no plan for getting there. Don't push for sex the first night if he doesn't want it just because you love good sex. He might like to be charged by a team of wild horses, but he might like to be seduced slowly, with no sense of urgency. I tell my patients to think of every seduction as a Cecil B. De Mille epic. You first put big ideas in his head (Part I, the exposition), then you develop him (Part II, the development), then you make the arrangements to meet, for "perhaps more...?" (Part III, the climax, denouement, and the happy ending). I remind them that one reason they call them epics is that while they may take forever, they most always end on an upbeat.

Focused gay men also follow up on an initial contact. It never hurts to follow up your look with a good evening, or a simple hello, said with a warm accepting smile. Try to get his phone number if it's no for tonight, then make that call, and, if there is no one home, or a negative response at first, call again. Dick, a personal friend, met Ernie, they had wild sex, and Dick called Ernie back for more. But Ernie was too busy to see him, so Dick waited three months and called again, and still Ernie was too busy to make a date. So Dick forgot about Ernie, until Ernie called two years later. Now they are together in a committed relationship.

Seriousness

Forgetting that, as they say in the theatre, satire is what closes on Saturday night, too many gay men camp their way right past relationships.

In my opinion, too many gay men think that to find a lover it helps to be freaky. Recently on a TV show, the game host said to a contestant, "We've had people with nose rings, tattoos, and leather pants, but never all together." She replied, "I try to be the biggest freak I can." Again, another proof that bigger isn't always better.

Like her, too many gay men think it's a good idea to be flamboyant. They become flamboyant in nonsexual ways, as when they drive only BMWs in elegant resorts to make the important (to them) contrast with people who drive beat-up trucks with Labrador retrievers in the back, and they do it in sexual ways, as did one gay man who took his taxi driver home with him just so that he could tell his friends, "What a hoot, what a clever and wonderful and fabulous and original person I am, don't you agree, and wish you were me?"

Don't make silly jokes about gay relationships. They are not a joke, though they can easily be made into one. Jokes about gay relationships having a short half-life tend to trivialize something that you should be serious about. After all, your goal here is to be successfully paired for the long term. In like manner, adultery and divorce should be a source not of jokes but of concern. A hypomanic style cuts the pain, but it comes back because you didn't cure it.

Do not mug, cackle, scream, and otherwise become a satire on yourself—extremities tossed, facial expressions halfway between a smile and a grimace, loud hilarity belying the actual somberness of your present condition and future prospects. Stop what you are doing on a dime when you hear someone near you comment to his friend, talking about you, "A little louder Louise, and we will all dance to it." Do not give others the impression that you prefer a good laugh to a good lover. Do not humiliate people you are with by being the company they keep but don't want to be known by. Close the floorshow, refusing to put it on again unless you have actually been hired to be the entertainment.

Do otherwise, and people will rave about you, and invite you to all their parties, then fall in love with the quiet boy next door. Paradoxically, at least at first, you are most desired when you are least noticed. So fade into the woodwork, and instead of making being gay an opportunity to be unusual, make it the nonevent of the year. Blend into all that unexceptional scenery that lies on the side of the road to heaven.

Ralph, a patient of mine, was a specialist in smart remarks. Instead of making personal introductions work for him, Ralph mocked them as the work of a peasant matchmaker. A new acquaintance of Ralph's, a man from New Jersey, suggested they take a trip to the New Jersey countryside together, saying, "It should be lovely there," but Ralph put him down by saying, "It should be, but it isn't."

Though Ralph wanted a serious relationship, his humor and attempts to be clever distracted him from reaching his goals. Trivializing his pursuits and making a big joke out of everything was his way to hide. He did much better when he followed my suggestion that he close down the clever-line machine and say something simple and honest like: "I would like to meet you and see if something comes of this."

Humor and finding love sometimes do not mix. Humor can be used to hold people off, and you do not want to distance anyone when you are trying to build a relationship. Also, while a healthy sense of humor is a special and attractive human quality, jokes that hurt, humiliate, or demean others do nothing to advance a relationship.

As I asked Ralph, "When was the last time you heard of a clown being the hero of a romance novel?"

Sensibleness and Ordinariness

Sensible gay men are ordinary individuals who do not feel that being unexceptional represents a capitulation to the establishment. They don't choose to rebel, developing an eccentric identity with unique behavior that pulls them out of the mainstream where all the fish are jumping. These are the sensible qualities you should aim for and that anyone can achieve:

- Fall near the middle on a continuum between a shy shrinking violet and an intrusive Venus flytrap.
- Look neat without being sloppy or fussy. Be carefully negligent in your dress and perfectly bland in your presenting attitude.
- Act happy without being euphoric.
- Be calm without being withdrawn.
- Be assertive without being pushy.
- Be seductive but in a low-key and subtle way.
- Eliminate, or at least cover up, neurotic tendencies such as talking too much, worrying out loud, or telling the same story over and over again.
- Don't have fixed, sharp-edged identities that you put between yourself and the world.
- Don't unfurl the pennant you carry to remind yourself, and everyone else, of the great place you have prepped and what an important, good boy that makes you.
- Be quietly tucked away somewhere in an emotional and physical culdesac, preparing the house for the visit of that solid citizen of your dreams.
- Do not be a novelty item that people soon lose interest in.
- Prefer a pleasant weekend shopping to a frantic night on the meat rack.
- Stay away from the leather sling in preference for bread-and-butter sex, which, like bread and butter itself, goes with almost everything.
- Recognize that the waiter is cute but the customers are also available.
- Hate the way the Cinderella story goes, thinking it's insane trying to get anywhere walking in glass slippers.

Hank, one of my personal friends, announced to anyone who would listen that he no longer liked New York because all the small stores were being pushed out by the big chains, then added that he felt no gym worth attending because he didn't like the gym culture. Brilliant Hank was saying all this to a man he just met who loved New York, adored shopping in Kmart, went regularly to the gym, and was looking for a companion to accompany him to these places.

Empathy

Empathic gay men show real interest in that new man they are talking to. Instead of talking about yourself, focus on him, and become a loving and admiring audience. Ask him questions to find out what he likes, both in and out of bed. Listen to the answers without asking him to repeat himself because you didn't hear him the first time. Stop trying to impress him. Don't be selfish and demanding, and reciprocate so that if he buys you a drink you buy him one back.

Creativity

Be a creative person who can have an intelligent discussion with someone right from the start, making it clear that with all your skills you are not just a perfect clothes dummy or just great in bed, but also are going to be good around the house, in all its rooms, and that if they get involved with you they will get a talented person. If you are not natively talented, develop what talents you have, and get new ones.

Contemporaneousness

Live in the present. Do not be like David, an old friend, who, every time someone comes over to him, steers the conversation around to his favorite movie, *The Women*, from decades ago, because that movie takes him back to a more enchanting time of his life. If you look to the past it is only to make the present more enticing—not, "I just love Joan Crawford's movies—they don't make movies like that anymore," but, "The plays I write take their inspiration and structure from the classical works of William Shakespeare." Nostalgia makes for a self-fulfilling pessimistic view of the here and now. Send a more positive message, and send it to present company.

Preparedness

Know what to do when things begin to happen. Have a dating drill like a fire drill, so that you don't drop the ball and screw up something good. Practice saying "yes" (one "s" only) so that you are always ready for, and able to handle, that unexpected opportunity that comes your way.

Sobriety

Do not drink heavily or use nonprescription or prescription medications improperly. Curiously, some have many paradoxical effects. They make you too relaxed to solve your problems, while giving you too many problems to solve while you are so relaxed. Arthur was taking Valium and Prozac to control his anger. Rather than keeping his anger in check, the drugs were suppressing it without eliminating it, so the anger built up inside, and regularly emerged in the form of blowups, hurtful both to him and others.

Now that you have climbed Step Seven, you are as desirable as you are cute. But there is still another challenge to be met. How do you stand out above a crowd of cute and desirable men, so that you can get him to notice, and turn him on to, you? That's Step Eight, worming your way into his heart.

8

Step Eight: Worm Your Way into His Heart

In this step, I will show you how to use applied psychology to further your legitimate ends. My strategy involves win-win methods where you read individuals and work the room, creating a desired positive response instead of leaving things up to chance. My method is designed to help you go beyond simply reacting to your environment to get to the point where you make your environment react to you.

Win-Win Methods

By using win-win methods, you can get close to someone who might otherwise elude you, either because he didn't notice you, or because he did notice, but rejected, you. I am not suggesting that you use people. Rather, I am suggesting some methods you might employ to bring men around to accept and welcome you—for the benefit of you both. I don't mean sending flowers to someone you are not interested in just so that you can get him to offer you a room in his centrally located apartment, or using sex as a source of funds. I mean grabbing a man's attention and turning him on using a series of maneuvers that effectively catch his eye, change his mind, and capture the heart and soul of someone who might otherwise pass you by.

Get to Know Your Customer

Develop a thoughtful, rational approach to meeting him based on what facts you can gather by observing him for a while yourself. Ask yourself, "Is he my type?"

and, "Do I want him?" Also ask yourself, "Does he look receptive tonight or does he appear to be remote, preoccupied, restless, or angry?" Then ask others who know him what he is like. Ask, "What's the story with that one?" "Do you think I have a chance with him?" and, "What, if anything, can I do to improve my chances with that man?"

Learn How to Read His Mind

Inferring, or trusting your intuition, is not only an elusive talent you are born with; it is also an ability you can develop over the years by testing your gut reactions to see if they align with reality, as determined by follow-ups. The ability to intuit and infer helps you identify and sort important clues as to what kind of personality he has, what he might be thinking, and how he might be reacting. It helps you guess his *preferences*, that is, what might turn him on and off. Now you can say and do what you think he will respond to. For example, intuition helps you know who to play hard-to-get with, and who to come on strong with. You should play hard-to-get if you think he is one of those men who find distant remote people fascinating, not exasperating. For example, Mel, a patient, just loved a cute waiter in a gay restaurant when the waiter was cool and remote. Then the waiter made the mistake of befriending Mel too aggressively, and Mel didn't like him so much any longer, because for Mel the mystique and challenge of the relationship were gone. In contrast to Mel, many men are exasperated by men who play hard-to- get. This is especially true for men who are shy and sensitive to rejection. Such men are likely to interpret remoteness as disinterest.

In my experience, a good rule to follow is: while ignoring masochists turns them on, ignoring narcissists turns them off. What about being assertive? Not if you want to seduce the person who is afraid of getting close. What about being controlling? It works with some men—they wouldn't make human dog collars if no one liked to grovel. But it doesn't work at all with men who are disaffected and rebellious.

Be sexually aggressive? Not with an idealistic man who needs to overvalue you. Many times, even the most flamboyant gay man wants a virgin lover. Sexually repressed themselves, these men tend to be turned off by flamboyant sexuality in others. They prefer men who don't have an obvious "past." Some even want you to act as if you are straight. For them, sex is sexier when understated and implied, not screamed. For such men, true love is pure and asexual. Find a way to say to such a person, "I will confine my sexuality to you," without seeming to be a prude. Be a neovirgin, about to be deflowered by *him* and *him* alone, even though your time is long gone for his being the first one, and the best you can do is grow new buds next season. Don't be dishonest about it. Everyone knows the truth. But don't act like just another animal in heat. That can break down his harmless fantasies and illusions.

Know a Potential Partner's Emotional Needs and Problems

Knowing a potential partner's *emotional needs* helps too. Doing that makes you look terrific in his eyes, however pedestrian you look in your own. All men view you, at least in part, from the distortive lens of past experiences and present fantasies. For example, most of us have heard something like, "People carry all this emotional baggage around with them and one of their heaviest burdens is having their parents on their back, and in their bedroom." True, having them on his back and in his bedroom can be his liability. But you can turn his liability into your asset.

We are all familiar with how often people fail in love with their therapists. That happens even when the therapists aren't physically attractive. It's called positive transference, and there's no reason why you cannot create it in him and direct it to you. Try being his mother. Everyone on some level thinks his mother is beautiful. This trick has been used by older men for ages because older men know, "Who else but an older person can do that job so well?" You know all those gorgeous young movie stars married to older men? You know all those couples where the younger man is good-looking and his older partner isn't particularly? If you are the older man, you can get the same thing for yourself, if that is what you want, by being motherly, which is one of the greatest aphrodisiacs of them all. It's not hard to be motherly. It's often enough to be interested in, and kind and loving to, him.

Knowing a person's *emotional problems* can help too. Do a quick personality profile. As Charles Keating says, speaking of ways to deal with difficult people, it helps to understand the syndromes of others. Syndromes are patterns of behavior that go beyond emotional needs to suggest and outline emotional difficulties. Knowing the syndromes gay men have can give you a strategic edge—and I describe the most common of these based on my clinical experience as a psychiatrist who has seen enough patients to know how you can make other people's emotional baggage work for you. It's not that complicated. For example, Saul, one of my patients, seeing John's hang-dog look, recognized that he was depressed, so he decided to approach him gently and slowly, working on improving his self-confidence by complimenting him and easing his guilt about sex by affirming his interest in him as a person, not devaluing him as just another fling. Here is a quick, hardly infallible rundown of possible nervous types, offered as a general guide for how to behave with a "new recruit." None of the suggestions below either guarantee success or suggest reasons to steer clear. However, do take these ideas into consideration in deciding who you choose to approach and what opening gambits you might try. Actually, these suggestions are, selectively of course, worth a try even with people who are perfectly healthy, or just slightly neurotic about things in general. Because everyone is a bit neurotic, everyone will like you better if you speak to their universal anxieties and fears.

Paranoids

Paranoids are identifiable by their shifty glances and tendency to recoil when approached. They also get a reputation for being cold and distant, making others wonder why they are in the bar, or anywhere else in public, in the first place.

Don't startle a paranoid; be very gentle. A paranoid should be reassured from the start that you are not out to enforce the sodomy laws or otherwise hurt, devalue, or attack him. Paranoids love people they feel safe with, and they feel safest with people who don't challenge them right away, or otherwise move too quickly.

Depressives

Depressives are identifiable by their slumped shoulders, downcast expression, and pessimistic views and attitudes, either expressed or implied. Don't devalue a depressive; affirm him. A depressive needs to be given confidence from the first word out of your mouth, as in, "I would be pleased to meet someone as handsome as you." Also, to avoid seeming to be rejecting, be clear: "I am available."

Narcissists

Narcissists are identifiable by their noses up in the air as they tilt their heads to heaven, all the better to hear and receive their next order from on high; that look of exquisite boredom on their faces; and a self-centeredness as reflected in a conversational preoccupation with "I" as distinct from "you," or anybody else.

Don't criticize a narcissist, and even a little fawning may not hurt. A narcissist should be flattered from word one: "Love that tie, love those shoes." Don't argue with a narcissist either. Don't ever argue with anyone, as a matter of fact, because everyone has enough narcissistic tendencies to dislike someone who gives them an argument, crossing and hurting them. Just recently, I suggested that a dog that was barking at our dog on the street was hostile. His owner, rather rudely I thought, suggested another possibility: "My dog never gets angry; she is a good, sweet, loving dog; she is just disappointed that your dog isn't interested in nuzzling her." Both of us were right. Yes his dog was disappointed, and yes, being disappointed, she got pissed off and started barking like a little bitch. But who was right wasn't what counted. I was hurt that he started in on me.

Hypomanics

Hypomanics are identifiable by their shellac-cutting cackle, their motor mouth, their hypersensitivity paradoxically combined with insensitivity to others, and their pervasive but inappropriate optimism in the face of all evidence to the contrary.

Don't cross a hypomanic. Instead, go along with the general hilarity. Join in the frantic fun, the rough equivalent of, "Let's all dance." Yes, this bar is a wonderful place, the men here are gorgeous, the world is your dance floor, and there's even a disk jockey in heaven with the disco beat just waiting for you to come up and boogie.

Obsessive-Compulsives

Obsessive-compulsives are identifiable by their prissy ways with napkins, swizzle sticks, toothpicks, martini olives, beer-bottle labels (they like to pick them off down to the bone), and dust on the barstool.

Obsessive-compulsives just love it when you leave room for uncertainty. Words like, "perhaps," and phrases like, "If you wouldn't mind," and "Is it okay that…?" make the best come-ons and avoid some of the worst turnoffs. Instead of, "Let's get out of this place and go home together," say, "If you aren't busy tonight, perhaps we can leave together and take a little walk to wherever you might like to go, or if you are busy tonight perhaps we can arrange something for tomorrow night or even next week, or whenever you are free." Exhale.

Histrionics

Histrionics are identifiable by their outlandishness, with minds like platform shoes—high but not mighty, and their cataclysmic overreaction, positive and negative, to trivial things, as in, "Isn't that jacket just *fabulous?*" or, "Aren't those just the *ugliest* shoes in the whole world?"

Don't fail to applaud a histrionic, and use the word "fabulous" a lot, applied to him, and to everything else too. Think of him as someone who has just sung the "Bell Song" from *Lakmé* and is now reemerging from the wings to take one more bow. Ogling and admiring him makes him feel important, so put that spotlight on him and shout bravo and keep on applauding right through all the curtain calls.

Staying one down is often best with highly competitive histrionic men. They not only want their name up in lights, they demand top billing too. I hear your protest already. I want to be me, that is humiliating, an identity killer, an unacceptable compromise, and think of what it might do to my self-esteem. Yes, you are absolutely right. But you have to remember that we are not talking about self-fulfillment or of character development. We are talking about getting involved with Mr. Right, and the two things are most definitely not the same. Don't turn this kind of man off by coming on strong. Coming on weak is a much better idea, at least for now.

Conversely, if you are a highly skilled person and you are dismissed by a histrionic man, though it is hard not to feel rejected, don't. Don't say to yourself, "I cannot see why he rejected me—I have it all." Instead say to yourself, "He rejected me *because* I have it all." Just tell yourself that a bus can only have one driver, and try someone else.

Sadists and Masochists

Sadists are identifiable by their tattooed-on bumper stickers, that is, body art displayed for all to see. They are also known for their chains, boots, and other rawhide accessories, and for their tendency to favor aggressiveness above overassertiveness.

Masochists are identified by the all-suffering look they exude that informs you that they have been hurt before and are now offering you a second chance. Also notable is their tendency to make themselves the butt of cruel jokes and put themselves down, not like depressives because they want a second, more positive opinion that offers hope and support, but because they want you to agree with their negative self-evaluation and respond critically, punitively, and in a way that humiliates them.

At least symbolically, be a sadist to his masochist or a masochist to his sadist. Sadists like men who tolerate and even thrive on cruelty. Unlike histrionics, masochists like the dark rather than the spotlight, and people who are critical of, not complimentary toward, them.

A patient of mine, who happened to be a doctor, always used to say, "I hate sirens. When I hear one and I am at work, I think it is an ambulance, I am getting a new admission through the emergency ward, and I won't be able to get out to the bars before they close. And when I am in the bars, I think it is a police car coming to raid the place, and I will be locked up and won't be able to get back to work the next morning."

Standing in a bar in Chicago during the height of the era of police raids on the local bars, my patient thought his worst nightmare had just come true. Perhaps he oozed fear, or a desire to be punished, because this really handsome man walked over to him and said, "I'd like to meet you." To that my patient responded, "And I would like to meet you too." The man then announced he was the police, took him by the collar, and pulled him off into a corner of the bar. Shaking with terror he awaited his captor's next move and the arrival of the paddy wagon, only to have his captor tell him he really did want to meet him and that what he just did was all a big joke. Then he invited him to go home with him.

This man who pulled this stunt got to be the famous newscaster he was partly by knowing his customer. He somehow knew that my patient would go for this sadomasochistic act, and rightly sensed from the start that the heart-stopper in the bar would set the scene for the heart-stopper still to come.

Be the Best Possible Manipulator You Can Be

An *evil* manipulator is one who is out to make a fast buck. He is a con artist, like a man who seduces cute eighteen-year-olds by promising them the moon even if that was telling a lie. He didn't actually have to be a tycoon of industry just because he said he was, because by the time the kid found out the truth, the sex was over and it was too late to take it back.

An *inept* manipulator plays games with relationships only to have them backfire. He follows such advice as, "Never accept a Saturday night date past Tuesday," (Not even if you met him Wednesday?) or "Set him loose, and if he comes back to you then he is really yours." (If you want to test out the validity of that theory, try it with your parakeet.)

He might keep two men on the hook, playing one off against the other while he decides between them, only to have them fall in love with each other—just like in the movies. Or he might use his looks to lure rich and powerful men into giving him a place to live, only to discover, after being thrown out after sex, that he sold his body for nothing. Forgetting that mixed feelings lead to mixed results, instead of making up his mind one way or the other and either going for, or staying away from him, he ogles someone then doesn't follow through. He teases, zagging when the other zigs, looking at him, then not saying a word and not moving a muscle when he looks back. That turns people off not only directly but also indirectly—the latter because other people see you doing it, and flee for self-protection. This manipulator forgets that getting a reputation in the world of romance is as important as getting a reputation in the world of medicine.

In contrast, a *good* manipulator is not "out to make a fast buck" but is rather "out to make a buck fast." He is not a con artist, but rather is an artistic con. He is not out to get something for nothing from others, but to make sure others don't miss that great opportunity to get something from him.

A good manipulator catalyzes relationships. A man who lives across the way from us sits on his stoop with his large parrot, which he uses to attract the attention and admiration of passersby. They stop and fawn over the parrot, and who knows how many people he meets this way

We have a paralyzed dog and we walk her in her little wheelchair (really a little cart). Everyone stops to talk to us and to ask what is going on. I cannot help thinking, "What a great idea! If you are single and if only the dog wouldn't mind (it certainly would!) you could get a regular dog, put it in a wheelchair, and walk it, just to meet people."

One of the oldest tricks there is involves walking a normal dog as a lure to get to meet other dog lovers. Of course, don't get a dog just for that purpose, but if you already have one make it take care of you. Dogs cannot talk, but they can say something nice about you, as you get points for liking animals. So relax, forget about coming up with clever opening lines, and let your dog come up with those great opening lines for you.

Here's an example of a practical catalyst, one that almost everyone, or at least everyone without too much shame, can try. A gay student who had very little money used to stick his drink out in the path of someone he was interested in when the person was passing by. The drink got knocked and spilled, and sometimes in the process the conversation got started, and he even got a free refill, too. A good manipulator will shoot for a man's fetish, or any other emotional problem he detects in others and knows how to speak to. Hustlers know this manipulation very well. They are natively clever about their shoes, or which body parts they expose and which they keep hidden.

A good manipulator will certainly play to a man's ego. All people, not just gay men, have narcissistic qualities. They love an audience. They like people who see them as important and wonderful. They like others to be subordinate. So, compliment him freely and let him prevail over you—at least in all the unimportant things, and for now.

Positioning yourself right is a kind of manipulation—what therapists call an "environmental manipulation." Go where a few good men are. That often involves trying the geographical solution. That consists of changing your surroundings for a purpose. You might move from a small town to a large city, or from a peripheral part of a large city to the center of town, like Pat did when he moved from the northern tip of Manhattan to the Lincoln Center area just to be near all the action. Mark, stuck in a rural area where being gay led to social isolation due to the lack of possibilities, changed his luck simply by going to the big city, where there were more opportunities. Geographical solutions are different from geographical wandering, where you move just to get away from it all. Frank felt stuck in the anonymous city of New York, and ran off to San Francisco where he thought the people were friendlier and the dating scene better. He discovered that all he had changed were his address and telephone number.

Try Ploys

A ploy is a minimanipulation, and it can be dishonest (bad) or honest (good). Here's an incident from my past that illustrates a dishonest ploy. Because we had the same first name, at a party someone once mistakenly thought I was Mart Crowley, the author of the play, *The Boys in the Band*. He told a friend of his I was, and it got around, making me instantly popular and in more demand than I ever have been, or probably will ever be, again!

Here are some honest ploys to try:

- Be a good listener. Open the conversation, turn off your motor mouth, then step back and hear what he has to say.
- Spill a little of your drink and clean up after yourself, to attract attention to yourself (and to get the sympathy vote).
- Make your availability known. Broadcast your desires so that others don't have to guess what you want. Let everyone know, "sotto voce," that you are available. Be like those people who send out one thousand pieces of junk mail so that there might be one positive response. How can others find you, or find you a lover, if they don't know you are looking?
- Pick someone who is reading or writing and ask him about the book he is looking at or the notes he is taking.
- If you go out to eat alone, go to a place where you can eat at the bar, not at a table. That way someone can approach you without making a big show of it.

Be Alert, Calculating, and Bold

By calculating, I mean do the math. Relationships are not so special that there are no rules for success or failure. In fact, the same rules apply here as everywhere else. Relationships are tradeoffs. Think of what you can give him in exchange for what you might get back. Drop a few hints along the way—connections in the artistic world, many friends, and all the sexual favors too. As for being bold, I myself would rather lose a lover knowing I did all, and pushed as hard as I could, than lose one after playing hard to get, something that I will always think backfired.

Work Hard

Don't become naïve and careless, expecting things to work out for you, without your having to work on them. Success in relationships is like success in writing a novel. It involves 80 percent perspiration, 10 percent inspiration, and 10 percent having the luck to find someone in the audience who knows how to read. Don't expect relationships to fall into your lap. Make a lap for them to fall into.

Be Careful

Avoid stirring up negative instead of positive feelings about you. If something doesn't work out, no big deal, but you don't want to make a bad mistake with someone potentially dangerous. Once, Saul was walking between bars in New York City when he saw this nice-looking man walking next to him. He jokingly stuck out his thumb as if he were asking him for a ride. The man responded by calling for a few buddies and asking them to help him mess Saul up. You can try to break through the straight façade, but make sure you have an escape route if there is a structural collapse.

If this all seems like a lot of work—it is. Developing relationships is not all fun. It's also serious business. It requires your full attention and commitment. You have to get up early in the morning (really stay up late at night) to do it. It takes motivation and sometimes courage too, and a willingness to sacrifice and endure. But in the long run it is worth it.

Now that you are cute, presentable, desirable, and noticed, are you home free? Not quite yet. Being human, it's likely that you will climb Step Eight only to stumble and fall—because you have hit an internal obstacle to joy and success. In Step Nine, which you will no doubt have to climb more than once, you will learn how to overcome the obstacles of fear of committing, inertia, loneliness, love-aversiveness, and the human capacity to be distracted from long-term goals by all the unimportant things in the form of short-term pleasures. This is a big step for you to navigate, but once you reach the top of this step, you can see the horizon even better and that new man you are looking for in even clearer focus.

9

Step Nine: Overcome Obstacles

Up to now, in Steps One through Eight, you have been learning what to do to move forward looking for love. Now I describe some things that might be holding you back. You will learn how to break free from what might be strait-jacketing you. Almost no one moves in a straight line toward a predetermined goal. It's usually a matter of backing and filling, where, like a soldier retreating for the moment, you deal with obstacles in your forward march by making yourself stronger, regrouping your forces so that you can sally forth and try again, and again, until you win first some battles and then the war.

Fear of Commitment

Some gay men who say they want to be single are choosing a reasonable option in life. Marriage isn't right for everyone. For example, there are generational preferences, with the desires and ideals of a twenty-year-old expectedly different from those of a sixty-year-old. But many gay men say they want to be single when they are in fact:

- buying into myths about what is good, right, and possible in gay life based, for example, on the false belief that gay relationships never last;
- being political, basing what they want for themselves on what personal behavior will do the most for the reputation of gays as a group;
- feeling too anxious to make wise decisions or act on them, or so depressed that their blue mood serves as a wet blanket; or

- using a desire for distance to hide a fear of closeness.

Yes, it's true that marriage isn't right for everyone and that there is no one right way to live. And it's true that there are actually some advantages to being single, or at least persuasive excuses for not committing. For example, Paul spoke of the advantages of always being able to find the scissors he was looking for, and there were certainly some.

However, many of my patients who told me that they were happy being single really weren't. They were simply saying, having decided, based partly on experiences they had in the past, that it was just too much trouble, too painful, or too hopeless to even contemplate a committed relationship. They were the fox, and committed relationships were their very special bunch of sour grapes. They hadn't decided what they wanted out of life. Something inside of them had decided it for them.

For example, when Paul, one of my patients, and I took the time and trouble to rethink his position about the wonders of being single, he discovered that his so-called preference was really an expression of fear. Paul, as is true of so many gay men like him, said he preferred being single when he actually feared closeness and commitment, and was citing the undeniable advantages of being single to rationalize that fear, adjusting to something he felt he couldn't have, and avoiding something he felt he couldn't handle. Paul insisted over and over again in therapy that he absolutely didn't want to get married. One day it slipped out that in a particular situation he just couldn't say, "I love you," even though that was exactly how he felt. He said he didn't like a certain man because the man was pushing him too hard to become his lover. It became clear that Paul wanted to be his lover but dreaded being wanted. Paul was really running with those scissors.

Gay men who try to convince themselves that it is good to be single, when in fact they really fear getting married, typically give their true feelings away by protesting too much. They explain their desire to be single in great, and unnecessary, detail, as if by convincing others of all the advantages they can convince themselves too. They have a long list of reasons for staying single:

- I can sit at home surrounded by the things I love.
- No one throws away the latest newspaper on me.
- I can always keep the bedroom at the temperature I like.
- I can grow on my own.
- I will never be pressured by a partner to change.
- I will never be rejected or abandoned by a partner.
- I will never have in-law trouble.
- I can have sexual variety.
- I can continue to enjoy dreaming of meeting Prince Charming—you can't do that if you have already met him, now can you?

Of course, not all single gay men who fear commitment express their fear of commitment as a desire to be single. Some openly admit that they want to get married, but convince themselves that they are single not by choice but because they have no alternative. They tell me that that's just the way things are today. They say there are no good single men left anymore. They say that they cannot find a lover in Chicago, or in Paducah, Kentucky, or anywhere (fill in the blank). They claim that they once had a bad experience with a relationship and they say that that is par for the course. They confidently announce that being gay and commitment don't go together. They say that now isn't a good time to look for a relationship because it's summertime in the city and too hot, fall when everybody is just getting back to work, winter when everyone is in Florida, or spring when people are just beginning to open up their summer homes.

I have reviewed these and other excuses with my patients. Together we considered that perhaps long-term, committed, monogamous relationships were not wrong for them; rather that they were wrong for long-term, committed, monogamous relationships. Then we worked together to make them right. In particular, we worked on their love-aversity.

Inertia

I can't tell you that a lover is for you, but I can tell you that having a lover works for me and that it is a great alternative to being single. I can also tell you that if you accept my premise and go for that lover you have been resisting, you will likely discover inertia. Inertia is a very powerful force that makes changing hard. All of a sudden, sameness seems mighty comfortable. Success is not guaranteed either. But an inherent property of inertia is that the harder you try to overcome it and the more you keep on keeping on, the more likely it is that you will succeed in breaking free of its grasp. Here are some specific steps you can take to overcome your inertia.

Prop Yourself Up Emotionally

An isolated earring or a delightful tank top in no way changes the fact that underneath the serene or self-aggrandizing façade some gay men present is the feeling that they are not entitled to be happy and successful. If you think you are worthy, you will be more inclined to take charge of and make changes in your situation, changes that reflect your true value, not some imagined fall from grace.

Of course, it is possible that you have a reason for feeling you are not entitled to the good things in life. You could, for example, be a bitchy hurtful queen. If that's you, please reform. But the majority of gay men are perfectly OK as they are, only they criticize themselves too severely and for little or no reason. If that's you, instead of doing things differently, view yourself differently. For one thing, stop magnifying your bad points. In particular, avoid vicious cycles where small self-criticisms demoralize you so completely that you are no longer in a position to forgive yourself for anything at all.

Develop a Plan of Action

The surest way to reach your goal is to have a plan of action. Here are some action-oriented things for you to try.

Be Clear About, Set, and Implement Long-Term Goals

Push yourself. When tempted to operate according to whim and passion, remember that in life impressionism makes good paintings but bad blueprints. Develop a disco philosophy. You love the tunes, why not live by the lyrics? For example, keep dancing, and don't stop smiling, until you mend, mend, mend that broken heart.

Follow through from start to finish, from intention to design to fulfillment—without breaking the connection. The wheel that gets the grease (your relationships) is the wheel that stops the squeaking. Work hard at romance. Instead of a fatalistic attitude, accept that you make your own luck. Accept that there are some things you must do that are difficult, and some rules that you have to go by. Tolerate your successes without thinking you don't deserve them and without survivor guilt that makes you think of yourself as a bad person because you got something others can only dream about having, or because you think you have taken someone away from somebody else who really wanted or needed him.

Select, Don't Settle

Avoid adjusting to something you think you cannot change. Adjusting to circumstances that are really under your control is just a cop-out. When you have a real problem, fix the problem, not yourself. For example, if you function better in the city than in the suburbs, forget about becoming a soccer guy, and just move.

Model Yourself after Those Who Have Been Successful

Discover what people who have survived and succeeded are like, and how they did it. Then do what they did. Usually, you will find that successful people were willing to work hard at finding relationships. Imitate the relentless ones who refused to be stopped until they got what they started out for.

Stick with Positive People

Avoid people who don't like to see you happy or successful because they are competitives who hate people who do better than they do, dependents who don't want to lose you, or people in misery who love company. Buying into what negative gurus think causes you to break your stride. Especially avoid those who act like omniscient doomsday seers when they are, in fact, more like grandmothers steeped in ancient but no longer relevant tradition, who always know the one right way to do things, while discouraging you from doing things right. For example, don't be too willing to buy into the meant-to-be reassuring bromide that committed relationships aren't right for everyone. That is often intended to comfort those who cannot have such a relationship by telling them that they are okay as they are and that things are okay as they stand. That's a good philosophy when there is no real, or at least no real immediate, chance of improvement, but it's a bad one when things could be better, when instead of living with pain you should be taking just what the doctor ordered for you.

Play your cards close to your chest. Don't give negative people the ammunition they need to shoot you down. Don't confess your mortal sins to someone who disses anyone just because he is less than immortal.

Act on Faith

Give having a committed relationship a try. If you don't mind my bossiness, just do it for me. After all, you can always break up and go back to living alone once more. But I think that once you have tasted the pleasures of long-term love, you will never want to go back to being by yourself again.

Exercise

Exercise helps both directly by reducing lethargy and indirectly by improving your self-image and your body, while simultaneously bringing you into contact with people you might want to meet.

Consider Getting Professional Help

If trying to talk yourself out of your inertia, undermining the excuses you give yourself to stay the same, and otherwise dealing with yourself on an emotional and practical level aren't enough to get you moving, you might need to seek professional help. See a therapist if you recognize yourself in the descriptions so far, yet cannot face up to and break through the kind of resistance that has become ingrained.

In conclusion, decide (1) if you like being single, don't feel bad that you are, and really want to stay detached and removed, in "splendid isolation," or (2) if for you the decision to remain single is not a decision, a solution, or preferred lifestyle, but a fear masquerading as a wish. Realize that fears about connecting, committing, and closeness make it very difficult to decide what you want to do with the rest of your life and with whom, and lead to counterproductive actions like opting for what is, in effect, a self-imposed exile.

Decide to leave familiar territory behind even if that means abandoning a place you know, and have come to love all too well.

Cut through the various layers of rationalization and denial to finally accept that a lover is exactly what you want. Decide to look for one, right now. Get started on your mission and see it through without aborting it before completion. Be persistent and patient and accept the need to relinquish some of your favorite philosophical positions, especially those related to personal identity, where wanting to be "me" can so readily keep you from wanting to become "us."

Loneliness

Loneliness is an obstacle to success when it hurts so much that you just give up and retreat. It is also an obstacle to success when it makes you impulsive and frantic to the point that, going about trying to connect in a panic, you do dangerous things sexually, abuse addictive substances, or make bad choices in men. I suggest some ways for you to deal with loneliness so that you feel good enough to look for love properly without being self-destructive or acting in counterproductive ways.

First, decide if you have Type A or Type B loneliness. Type A lonely gay men have long ago gotten used to being lonely, and even come to like it. If you are one of these men, you might say, "It's wonderful sitting home alone with my two cats and my inanimate possessions, the things I love." You might quote great poems written about the pleasures of being solitary, forgetting that some of these have been written by unhappy poets. You might cite, and even write, articles about the wonders of being by yourself. Like men trying to justify being single, you will probably hear yourself trying to talk yourself into believing that being alone is great because you can do what you want to do when you want to do it, and with whom, without someone being dependent on you, controlling you, envying what you have, and being jealous of who and what you get. Also like men trying to justify being single, you will likely emphasize how great it is to be free from family strife, for example, "No worry about mothers-in-law with teeth harsher than a serpent's." You play mind games to convince yourself that you are fine, dwelling on the subtle differences between being alone and being lonely to fool yourself into thinking that just because you are alone doesn't mean you have to feel lonely. Perhaps you even contrast your terrible childhood, where others bothered you just by being there, with your wonderful present, a paradise simply because everybody lets you be.

To an extent you are right. Loneliness isn't a matter of life and death, and it does have a few good things going for it. But whatever its advantages, and however great its delights, in my opinion loneliness should never be allowed to become a way of life. Men who have made peace with being lonely should start up the war with it again. First, give up trying to convince yourself that everything is OK as it is. Next, make your loneliness work for you. Use your down time to plan how to meet someone. Then make your moves, starting today.

Type B lonely gay men don't feel less lonely than they should. Instead, they feel lonelier than they need to feel. If you are a Type B lonely man, what you need to do is ask yourself, "Are things as bad as I think they are?" and, "Am I really as lonely as I believe I am?" You need to put what seems like intolerable loneliness into perspective so that you can handle it correctively and without panic. Here are some of the more helpful things you can do in that realm.

Be Rational and Realistic

Being rational and realistic about your present status and current condition starts with recognizing that since you didn't get lonely overnight, you won't get better overnight either. Look beyond the present, and keep your entire life in perspective.

Be Patient

Remember that men looking for relationships generally don't find them immediately. Not meeting someone tonight doesn't mean that you will never meet anyone at all. Thinking that makes everything look hopeless. Lonely gay men are in the same position as people waiting for a bus. It feels as if the last bus departed long ago. But wait patiently and long enough (and don't do something counterproductive like grabbing the first bus that comes along even though it doesn't go where you want it to) and you will be on your way. Sit back and relax. Nothing really bad can happen to you today just because you are lonely. You have time. Loneliness is more like the rust that corrodes than the fire that guts.

Don't Act Out of Desperation

Don't get frantic, hoping to connect at any cost. If you try that, you can lose your self-respect and hurt yourself both professionally and personally. Panic is good to the extent that it overcomes inertia. Panic is bad to the extent that it creates a crisis atmosphere. You cannot delay too long; on the other hand, you cannot rush into things.

Hasty action, sexual and otherwise, can be the enemy of finding just the relationship you need to overcome your loneliness. To the lonely man, love at first sight is a life raft, but since you aren't actually drowning, maybe you should wait for the cruise liner. If you have just broken up with someone, maybe your first reaction when meeting someone new is to sigh with relief. You are desperate to find a lover. You see all the married people about, and you want to be married too. You feel especially bad at those times when people are quietly together, like on Sunday morning. You feel your love life is going nowhere and nobody loves you either, which can be true, at least for now. At such times, your emotions run away with you and you think you are in love when you are not. You push too hard when you should be forbearing and patient, and you form fantasized love affairs with people you don't even know or like. It is like having an imaginary playmate, only for real. In desperation, you allow your judgment to bend and sometimes break. Taking it slow at such times and otherwise mastering your self-destructive passions is the order of the day. Difficult as it is, you must look around before you get married so that you don't have to look around afterwards.

Identify the Thoughts That Are Making Your Loneliness Worse

Identify the following damaging thoughts about loneliness and correct them. It will help you feel less pessimistic, and it will also help you develop better strategies.

Everything is all right. Yes, calming thoughts are good to have for now, but false reassurances can be bad for you in the long run. You are more likely to get out of this if you are realistic enough about your predicament to actually do something about it. When my niece's cat died, her grandmother told her that the cat was a star in heaven watching over her. The child felt better for now, and even asked for a telescope to see her cat. But what happens later when she realizes she was duped? Might it have been better to grieve for the old cat today and just get a new one tomorrow? I once complained to a psychiatrist I was seeing that I hated going to Maine all alone and rattling around in my small summer cottage all by myself. Trying to make me feel better about my present predicament, he waved his pudgy hand and looked up at the heavens with a big "aahhh," as if to say how wonderful it was communing with the little birds and watching the big sky. The happiest day of my life was when I sold that stupid little cottage and moved back to my own area, and instead of communing with nature started communing with the commuters.

If I am lonely now I will be lonely forever. As I just mentioned, loneliness feels permanent if you judge your life on a daily basis, like some people take their pulse every few minutes, or evaluate their long-term financial picture based on how the stock market did yesterday. Once, I was crushed with loneliness until I read a column in a gay-oriented paper that said that everyone the columnist knew in the same predicament found someone for himself within two years. It was so reassuring to know that it would be over eventually. I waited and it was—almost to the date. Is there any reason why that shouldn't be true for you?

The only gay men I knew who were lonely forever were the ones who down deep really wanted to be lonely, and that was strictly for reasons of their own.

It's not my fault, all gay men are lonely. Blaming gay life is displacing blame onto external circumstances believed to be beyond your control. Displacing blame, like false reassurances, cuts two ways. The good news is that you feel less depressed because you feel less responsible for your terrible life. Your reasoning goes: I don't blame myself for being lonely, it's my circumstances (fate, stars, bad luck, malignant lovers of the past, bitch-mothers of the present, etc.) This starts out to be reassuring! It is reassuring to blame the world instead of blaming yourself because you feel less responsible, and as a result you feel less guilty. But sooner or later, instead of feeling guilty you feel hopeless. Now the bad news begins. You feel more depressed because you feel that since you aren't the problem, you can no longer control the situation, take charge of your life, and come up with a solution.

In truth, gay or straight, you are mostly in control of, and responsible for, what happens to you. A corollary is that what happens to you is the direct result of what you did to yourself yesterday and plan to do to yourself tomorrow. And that is the really good news, because while you cannot change the world, you can change yourself. When it comes to being lonely today, self-defeating behaviors and poor tactics of yesterday are usually the problem—and that is a problem that usually has a solution.

People who aren't alone like me are to be seriously envied. Just because you are alone one Saturday night doesn't mean that you have to act like a waif out of Dickens, put your nose to the window of a gay restaurant where couples are eating, and turn jealous of all the revelers in there who have what you don't. I remember that when I was younger there was a time when I was so alone that I used to stare at the happy people inside. Relax. Like me, it's likely that you will eventually get what you want. Besides, I later learned that some of those happy couples I saw eating together, legs entwined under the table, were just having their last meal as a couple before the divorce became final.

Discover How Your Past Might Be Contributing to Your Present Pain

Analyze why loneliness is so threatening to you. Self-analysis helps you understand why you feel so lonely and get so upset about it. Look back over your life to see where the excessive pain associated with loneliness started, so that you can differentiate the present from the past. In my case, a special sensitivity to being alone in the here and now started when I was a child and my parents left me in the care of a senile, but still cruelly shrewd and scary, grandmother who hated me for coming between her and my mother. Day in and day out, she kept looking out of the window to inform me of the progress of the kidnappers who, according to her, were coming to get me. As I look back, it is pretty clear that her so-called fears disguised a secret wish. She wanted to have me spirited away so that I wouldn't come between her and her daughter, my mother. It helps me to remind myself that, being older, I am safe now, with not being kidnapped one of the advantages of not being a kid anymore.

Take Corrective Action

The best way to get over your loneliness is to do something about it even when you are only half-ready to act. Here are some things you can do to feel better quickly.

Start networking now. The way to meet *him* is to first meet *them*. Gradually, even ruthlessly, expand your circle of friends. Use the bars not to connect sexually but to connect personally. You are there to build a foundation. The superstructure will come later. For now, the concrete slab is the only thing that absolutely must get laid.

Follow a specific action plan. The following plan is derived in part from my own experience. I lost a lover to death when I was middle-aged and didn't meet Michael until nine years later. In the meantime, I had a series of abortive affairs, each of which felt like love when in fact each was a desperate striving to relieve loneliness. My experience taught me what not to do, and I pass on to you what I learned in the hope that it will help you act more wisely and effectively than I did.

The first mistake I made was to panic. Time was slipping by, it seemed faster and faster each year as I got older, and I acted out of desperation, feeling that I had to meet someone new before it was too late. The second mistake I made was to do nothing about the loneliness itself, and I mean absolutely nothing. I tried to fix the problem definitively by finding a new husband, but I never tried to deal with the problem directly by having a real life in the meantime. I ignored the fact that I had a lot of friends, a few good "sisters," and a loving family because, as I saw it, they were no substitute for having a lover. Indeed, I hardly saw them at all because I was busy kicking them over in my headlong rush to fall in love. As a consequence, I never went out to eat, didn't go to shows, didn't go to museums or art gallery openings, and certainly didn't tour the world by myself or even with friends, simply because I was unmarried. I didn't volunteer; I didn't join clubs; I didn't play sports; I didn't even work overtime because I feared that I couldn't stand the pace of being up all night cruising then having to face a long workday in the morning. Every waking moment was spent in thinking about and looking for Mr. Right. Before I could have a life, I had to have a lover.

My first real breakthrough came when I started going to the gym. This gave me both a means and a method for ending my loneliness. First, my body was improving, so I was becoming more desirable. Second, I was beginning to meet people at the gym, so I was developing a wider social circle. Third, my day was more scheduled. I had more to do than just sit around feeling sorry for myself waiting for the bars to get busy.

When I started going to the gym every evening and on weekends, my lonely life began to break into little, more manageable, pieces. The gym took an hour and a half each time. That meant that my day was now divided into two large pieces—BG and AG (before gym and after gym). Next, I broke off more and more pieces. I started going to the gay and lesbian center in my neighborhood, and playing bingo. Initially, I didn't like it there. It felt too much like a halfway house or a daycare center for people who have nothing better to do than rot, but I got over it, and onto what was important.

I learned that you shouldn't go home right after work on weekdays, then sit around drinking by yourself and watching TV. Instead, go somewhere first before going home. Go to an art gallery opening or a cooking class, shop for some new clothes, or go to a volunteer or second job. Do not hit the bars first before going home. Bar cruising at cocktail hour is perfectly dreadful. People come and go with groups from the office, are just trying to get over a bad day at work by having a few drinks to relieve the tensions, are delaying facing that lover they can't stand when they are completely sober, or are just too tired to be particularly responsive to meeting someone new.

Come weekends, which are very hard for some lonely gay men, you simply must have things to do you enjoy, even if you are doing them by yourself. Activities like adult education programs help break up the day. Visits to family can pass the time too and be pleasurable in themselves. Call up everybody you know and arrange to do things with them. Call not only other gay men but also straight people, and that means men *and* women. Stay longer at the gym as well, comfortable in the knowledge that you are building your future as you are building your body.

If you are the type who likes hard work, I recommend a second job. It takes up the slack, exposes you to new people, and provides you with what can be sorely needed income, for entertainment, gym dues, and those new clothes you will likely need to look your best for the Mr. Right you are searching for.

Reading helps a great deal too. Many gay men who are alone are just too agitated to sit quietly reading a book. But once you get into a book you get less agitated, a sense of calm comes over you, and you have at least a few peaceful hours. You are simultaneously improving your intellect and making yourself more special for that special person you are looking for in life. Take on a massive reading project. I recommend the *Decline and Fall of the Roman Empire*. Believe it or not, it's wonderful and sometimes hilarious, it takes forever to finish, and it shows you that there are people suffering and dying out there, which (not something I always recommend, but for now it might not be a bad idea) makes your problems with loneliness look, if not less important, than at least less momentous.

Consider getting professional help. In favorable circumstances, you can work out the emotional problems that might be causing you to be lonely—problems like love-aversion—on your own, with my help, or with some help from friends and family. In serious cases of loneliness, think about scheduling psychotherapy at least once, and perhaps twice, a week. That can help a great deal in desperate situations, in a number of ways. At the very least, psychotherapy sessions can structure the whole week for you. It is very calming to think, "I can survive, it is only a day and a half until my next session." Taking days, or weeks, one at a time is easier if the days and weeks are broken up into little pieces. Also, as my internist, Dr. Richard Wagman, says, having someone to talk to can allow you to correct misconceptions you develop on your own and etch the self-help experience in stone by making it more real intellectually and emotionally.

I've done a small survey of grief counselors and other therapists treating lonely people and discovered that they make the following basic points, which I summarize and pass on to you here. They tell their people of the pleasures of being by yourself for now. They tell them that going solo may not be the basis for a lifetime arrangement, but for now there are worse things, and the solo life has its own pleasures and advantages. (As I already mentioned, this approach can be counterproductive if it makes you satisfied with things as they are in a way that lessens your motivation to improve them.) They also tell their people that some of the pain of going it alone comes from feeling humiliated over not being with someone, the kind of feeling people get, and don't need to have, when they go into a restaurant and ask for a table for one. Self-blame for not having found a partner and the guilt associated with enjoying being unattached are two other potential sources of pain. If there has been a loss, particularly due to death, there can also be survivor guilt—about being happy and having things go better for you than for your dead lover, for instance. Finally, some therapists warn their patients not to develop the bad habit of getting too much pleasure from wallowing and luxuriating in distress. In my opinion, wallowing in your pain is a common and always bad mistake.

Fear of Rejection

Another obstacle in dating is fear of the inevitable rejections associated with trying to meet a lover. Many gay men are extremely rejection-sensitive, and some, virtually paralyzed as a result, hold back on looking for relationships in the belief that nothing ventured is nothing lost. If you have this problem, either you don't date at all or you date in such a way that nothing happens because you leave yourself so many escape hatches.

Most gay men would prefer to avoid experiencing rejection. They feel they would rather be lonely than to be hurt one more time. But it's a fact of life: dating is about the only way to meet a lover, and it necessarily exposes you to rejection. There are three possible methods for dealing with rejection:
- Avoid being rejected in the first place.
- Respond self-protectively to the inevitable rejections.
- Respond constructively and creatively to the inevitable rejections bound to occur by turning them into a positive experience, or, better yet, into an acceptance.

Avoid Being Rejected in the First Place

You can avoid feeling, and even being, rejected by fooling yourself into thinking that you don't care if you never meet anyone. You fear that no one will want you, and go to the opposite extreme and convince yourself that you neither want nor need a relationship. You stress the advantages of being promiscuous, and, as if to prove your point, you spend night after night in bars giving others the impression you want nothing more out of life than sex. This way you make sure that you don't get your heart broken. Besides, you win points in certain segments of the gay community for being as gay as you can be, which, as you see it, involves not taking yourself, or anything else, seriously. Of course, ultimately you suffer a great deal more because the desire for a relationship persists, no matter how much you deny it, so that all you have accomplished is to convert the fear that you won't succeed into the certainty that you will fail.

A better method of avoiding being rejected and getting your feelings hurt involves practicing safe dating. There are several ways to do this.

Be Selective about Whom You Approach in the First Place

Avoid starting or persisting in a relationship when you believe that the possible cost isn't justified by the results. Avoid being too assertive with an immoveable force, be quick to pull back and cut your losses if you sense things aren't going well, and be willing to close the books on a moment, or on a whole night, should you sense that there is no point in continuing.

Think Twice before Rushing Over to Someone in the Midst of an Attachment

Whether his attachment is romantic or otherwise, it's dangerous to fantasize that he will want you more than he wants what he already has, and that you will rescue him from that beast. Think twice about approaching someone who is part of a group obviously out together for the night. Approaching someone in a group puts the target of your advance in a difficult position. Because of his group loyalty, the easiest thing for him to do, even if he likes you, is to reject you rather than risk being inattentive to his friends over someone he doesn't even know. (However, don't forget the technique I first mentioned in chapter 7. When you sense that two men are just "sisters" hoping that someone will move in on them, it might not be a bad idea to try moving in on the shier and less handsome one of the two.)

Let Men Come to You

It can sometimes be beneficial to spend a night not approaching anyone, and instead focusing on the men who approach you. This, perhaps the most cautious approach of them all, doesn't protect you completely, because some men are teases who walk over to you as part of their plan to reject you. Also, perhaps more than any of the other methods in this category, this one reduces your chances of meeting someone by limiting your options to bold and assertive types.

Avoid Having a Rejection Mind-set

Rejection mind-sets tend to make what you expect and fear actually happen. People have a way of making their pessimistic expectations of the world come true. They have a way of proving their own points. If you think you are wasting your time, you just might walk over to someone to start a conversation then open on a sour note by putting yourself down. You might say, "You probably aren't looking for someone like me, but I thought I would give it a try," or use self-demeaning humor like, "My analyst told me to be bold, so I have chosen to start with you." You might even say something truly off-putting like, "Our eyes have met, but we haven't, yet."

Here's my rule: if you present yourself negatively, people see what you mean. If you present yourself positively, people wonder what they have been missing.

Respond Self-protectively to the Rejections That Are Inevitable

You might not be able to control what other people do to you, but you can control how you respond to them. You can become less sensitive, as if you don't care if you are accepted or rejected. However, there is a danger that not caring about being rejected can turn into not caring about being accepted.

A better and more helpful method in this category is to correct any illogical thoughts you might have about rejection. For example, a turndown is not a rejection. It's often just an "I" statement about what "I want," not a "you" statement about what "you have to offer."

Ask yourself this: was he really reacting to and rejecting me? Role-play for a moment. Think of yourself talking about other gay men who were basically strangers to you. Were you really evaluating them, or were you using a few minor and scattered clues they emitted to talk about yourself? Were you describing what they were or what you imagined them to be? In life, there are certain things we accept and certain things we deny. If you hurt your foot, you accept that you cannot run as well as before. But we don't always accept that getting older can mean not remembering as well as before, and we almost never accept that people blow us off not because they don't like us, but because they have problems of their own. You overlook significant realities when you are tempted to explain a rejection in strictly personal terms, forgetting that others' inner lives and current circumstances have everything to do with how they treat you.

As for their *inner lives*, others' problems invariably figure into the picture here. It often happens that people, gay or straight, reject other people as part of an emotional problem they themselves have. You think, "Look at him—isn't he beautiful" and then you think, "Look at him—isn't he wonderful," and then you think, "Look at him—he is so beautiful and wonderful that he must be sane." Yet, I know for a fact that some gay men in bars are seriously disturbed—because I see some of my disturbed patients in bars all the time. I realize that they are very good-looking and if someone cruises them and is turned down, they won't know how troubled they are and they will think they are being rejected when they are just being incorporated into a system of very personal beliefs. Some of my patients are hallucinating. Others have very seriously disturbed thought processes. I used to know one seriously troubled man who thought that when someone said, "Hello" he meant, "Too much sex!" It was hard to come up with an effective opening line for him! Still others are not very disturbed—they are just very ambivalent about being gay, or have been insular and independent all their lives. Still others are not disturbed at all. They are just acting out by going to a bar. They have had a fight with their lover and are there for spite. They are leading you on and then rejecting you because of their own ambivalence. They are eager to have you, but guilty about what they want, and, often with reason, afraid to get it because of what their lover might think, say, or do.

Many years ago, Farley, a friend, had a handsome coworker who practically begged Farley to have sex with him. Farley backed off, saying he was too busy because he was rushing to meet an important project deadline. Farley was also looking for an excuse to avoid sex with his coworker because he was in psycho-analysis at the time, "going straight," something in those days the psychiatric establishment felt was possible and desirable. Naturally, the coworker thought he was being rejected. How was he to know that Farley said "no" for very personal reasons—like compulsively needing to complete a project without interruption, and wanting to please his analyst and to prove to himself that his analysis was working and that he was going to wake up one morning, magically having become an avowed heterosexual? What the coworker didn't know was that instead of being rejected, he was being incorporated: right into Farley's serious inner personal conflicts.

As for *current circumstances,* a good possibility is that your so-called rejection was just a startle response. Being hit on can be intrusive and disruptive. You may simply have scared him by interrupting his reverie. Many people first have to recover from the shock of being approached before they can orient themselves to what is happening to them. Alternatively, he may be not responding to you simply because he is just dreaming of that nice weekend in the country with some-one he already met, or worrying about how he is going to pay his charge card bill this month, with your personal advances just reminding him of his cash advances. Maybe he recently had a bad experience. Once, two weeks after my friend John's lover left him, the lover's friend, Paul, approached John. It was a sincere attempt, but John was feeling generally "used" and didn't want to be used again—so he blew Paul off. The new man felt rejected, though he was merely a victim of John's circumstances.

Of course, someone you approach might say no because he believes that the two of you are mismatched, and he just doesn't want you. But even then the most likely possibility is that you are being turned down not because you are imperfect, but because someone else fits his bill better.

Another method in this category is to minimize the impact rejection has on you by attaching less importance to a rejection that has actually occurred. To do this, ask yourself a number of questions:

- Am I overreacting to a rejection because my self-esteem is already low? Is a rejection just another irrational reason for me to dislike and condemn myself?
- Can I really worry about what everyone thinks—in particular, someone I just plucked out of the air?
- How important in the infinite scheme of things is his blowing me off? Perhaps he did, but so what? How much does it really matter that a stranger doesn't want me?
- If he doesn't want me, so what? That's his loss, not mine.

Still another method in this category is simply to accept that you have been rejected, and go on from there. Dating, unless you are very passive about it, is inherently a dangerous act. You are out there, exposed, your ego ready to be bruised. After all, cold cruises are like cold sales calls. Sometimes they are rewarding, but they are unlikely to be productive most of the time. You are walking up to a stranger and putting your entire fate in his hands, at least for the moment. But you don't know this person, and he doesn't know you. It isn't always helpful, at least in the long run, to deny you were rejected, deny the importance of the rejection, or deny that it hurt using all the various ways suggested throughout my book, such as, "He didn't really know me," "It's his loss," and the like. Sometimes it is just better to accept the fact that you are not the man for every man, and get over it. Never go on to think: "Bad people get rejected, he is rejecting me, therefore I am a bad person." Just remember that no matter who you are, there is a fan club, and a website, for it.

John, a patient, felt that because someone rejected him no one liked him. He was in a bar looking for a lover. He saw a good possibility across a crowded room.

He screwed up his courage and said, "Hello, do you happen to know what time it is?" (The Supremes had the beat long before disco; Place is full of creeps isn't it?; Don't you wish you didn't have to do this at 3:00 A.M.?; What time do the bars close?; You look familiar, didn't we meet in another life?, fill in the blanks). John got rejected. He sulked, "This is all there is to life, isn't it. This was my test case, the one determining my basic value, wasn't it?"

Get over it, John. Just because a thread has pulled out of the skein of your life doesn't mean the fabric of your entire existence is going to fall apart.

- Stop overreacting. It might not have been a rejection, or if it was, so what, we all get rejected.
- Ask yourself if there is anything you can do to avoid a new "rejection."
- In your most confident voice, shout to yourself, "Next!"

A final method for dealing with hurt feelings is to devalue the person who hurt them. Bitchy queens do this all the time. They dish the world to make it a less hurtful place. Elsewhere I condemned dishing. Now I am suggesting that it's possible to dish by design, and that is what I am recommending here. Dish for a specific, calculated purpose. Be critical to help you get over a crisis of self-confidence. Use this method only in a serious emergency.

Turn a Rejection into an Acceptance

In a nutshell, turning a rejection into acceptance involves (1) being more persistent, and sometimes even pushy, and (2) turning a negative into a positive interaction.

Being *persistent* is worth a try for those of you who are not so shy that you cannot take the first step in approaching someone, yet so shy that you become quickly discouraged when you do not get the desired response, and retreat reflexively. I saw a patient who, whenever he spoke of his difficulties meeting people, said the same thing: "No one I say hello to says hello back." When I asked him, "Why don't you follow up the hello with, 'And how are you?'" he answered, "He rejected me once and he isn't going to do that again," or, "That's being too forward." He made a bad mistake by not turning a rejection into an acceptance by being persistent. He should have asked again, hoping he might change his mind after he had a chance to think about it.

A persistent gay man doesn't panic. You do not give up the pursuit too quickly, thinking failure is preordained because of how you look, or because you always have bad luck. You do not jump the gun, assuming rejection prematurely then rejecting first (as you see it, "back") in self-defense so that he doesn't have the satisfaction of rejecting you. You realize that no matter how good-looking you are, and how well you cruise, most of the time nothing happens. You go out night after night realizing that not every night out will be productive and that not every cruise will work the first time, or at all. And you hold the long-term view. You know that to make the paint stick, you first have to spend some time preparing the surface, and that while of course you are fading, it's a slow process and you have plenty of time before that tsunami wrinkle sinks all.

Being *pushy* means:

- Being bold and insensitive to the extent that it fits with your personality.
- Starting many conversations knowing that you will have to accept many rejections.
- Working on the same person a lot instead of making cruising a "wham bam thank you Sam" kind of thing and moving on whenever you see the first sign of trouble.
- Remembering that most people need to know you for at least a while before they can decide whether or not you interest them.
- Working on getting his full attention, knowing that with dating, as with real life, if you want someone you visit to answer the door you may have to knock more than once.
- Coming back to the same bar night after night, hoping he will be there, while looking more alluring each time, as if the changes in you are meant for him, so that you are not giving up unless the situation is

really completely hopeless, sometimes even hanging in there for months or years of trying.

Of course, being pushy tempts rejection and tempting rejection can throw you into a dating block, an impediment to action that is the emotional and practical equivalent of writer's block. In fact, the whole topic of dealing with rejection is handled well in many books on writer's block. Take a look at some of them.

In the realm of *turning a negative into a positive interaction,* some people who react negatively to you at first can be brought around if you don't reply negatively in kind. Instead, let them get some poison out of their system, accept their hostility, and wait patiently for the tirade to end, and your turn to respond, then meet their anger by being positive and loving.

In summary, many gay men constantly anticipate rejection to the point that they make lots of backup plans just in case the inevitable happens, then, imagining trouble even before it starts, default to these backup plans. If you are one of these men, you typically find yourself working your way up to a cruise then, to avoid having your feelings hurt, back off as soon as you sense the moment of truth is near. Or you give up completely to avoid ever experiencing failure.

Instead, follow these important suggestions for dealing with fear of rejection:

- Never let failure devastate you completely.
- Continue to try though you may not succeed.
- Try again and again if you fail, until you get the approach right or until you meet someone who likes you so much that he won't mind if you get it wrong.
- Chalk any failure up to experience.
- Recognize that if you are sincere, motivated, and ready, and don't keep yourself isolated, love will ultimately come your way—maybe not tonight, but eventually.

Unless you are extraordinary lucky, finding a lover takes courage, resiliency, a refusal to give in to one or even to many rejections, an awareness of how you sometimes provoke your own rejections, and an understanding that you haven't been rejected just because someone doesn't want you. It takes the realization that, if you have been rejected by someone, that someone isn't everyone, and the awareness that a certain man might not desire you not because you are bad but just because you aren't exactly what he wants.

Following these suggestions and accepting these basic premises and living by them doesn't assure you that you will overcome your fear of rejection entirely, for no one ever does. It certainly doesn't assure you that you won't be rejected. But it just might help you make important inroads into the problem, and possibly even solve it, if only because by trying hard you made something work by chance alone.

You might try keeping this book open to this section of this chapter, then going out and taking the chance that you might actually get yourself rejected. After a rejection, come back and reread this section, then go out and take another chance that you might actually get yourself rejected, and so on. That way, you both desensitize yourself to rejection and stir up some anxieties you weren't aware you had, exposing them to the light so that you can finally see them clearly and master them. Who knows? His response could even surprise you, either because your luck suddenly turned, or because your approach finally improved.

Love-Averse Behaviors

Gay men experience a number of emotional roadblocks that interfere with effective dating. As one gay man unable to connect after years and years of trying put it, "I like him, he likes me, and that starts a vicious cycle going." Different people have given different names to the behavior that is a combination of errors of omission and commission, and in turn a product of anxieties and fears about meeting a man, resulting in a fear of commitment and closeness. I call this group of behaviors "distancing," "removal," or "love-averse behavior." The different behaviors are united by a tendency to zig when he zags and to put your best foot forward, then shoot yourself in it. Thomas did just that when he left Boston and moved to San Francisco to be with a new lover, only to pick up stakes and flee back to Boston when the man suggested that the two of them live together.

It's easy to make fun of love-aversive men, or tell them to just cut it out, as if they are in complete control of themselves at all times. But it's important to recognize that they are often in severe pain. They feel guilty about being gay. They often reject others because they fear others might reject them first. Yes, their fangs are exposed, but they are exposed less for biting than for self-defense.

Here are some types of distancing behaviors. If you detect any of these distancing behaviors in yourself, or if you think you are removing yourself from love, you have to find out why and stop it promptly. Get your gut reactions and knee-jerk distancing responses under control.

Pissiness

Some men find themselves getting paradoxically annoyed when Mr. Right approaches. If this is you, you may think, "He is coming on to me too strong." You could think, "He wants me—what's wrong with that?"

You may think he is practically ordering you to go to bed with him, which is being pushy, or even rude. You could think, "Maybe I'll take that order and serve him up a little something nice, too."

You may think, "If I say 'yes' he will take over my life." You could think, "Maybe that's a great idea."

You probably get pissed off now because you got pissed off when you were a child under related circumstances. Seeing how that works might just be enough to stop you from getting annoyed and moving away from someone really nice. For example, Sam, a patient, only wanted elegant men right from a croquet match because they retroactively softened the shame he felt when his father wore his fishing shoes to Sam's bar mitzvah. Albert, forgetting that it's great to be wanted, felt anyone who came on to him was pushy, and pushy people turned him off, just like his parents did by never leaving him alone even when he begged them to get off his back. Naturally, these examples, being simplifications, don't fully explain these reactions. They do, however, exemplify the kinds of things that can leave a permanent mark on the lives of gay men, and make too big a difference in how they respond to positive overtures.

Fault-Seeking and Fault-Finding

Some gay men have a tendency to criticize and reject others, often the same way they criticize and reject themselves. They do this to others because it's what they got used to doing to themselves. They also do it to deal with feeling like a nobody compared to the man who has it all. Instead of improving themselves, they knock the competition. Lowering others' self-esteem makes things even, which makes them feel a lot better about themselves. Naturally, this scares people off. Most people don't like being hurt, and few people want an insult comic for a partner. Others also see through the compensatory nature of the behavior, as in, "He must feel like a big nobody if he has to put me down," and respond accordingly. When a third party is being dished to a second party, the second party usually recognizes, "I'm next."

Gay men who dish other gay men when they are supposed to be attracting them are participating in nothing. You simply must identify any overcritical tendencies in yourself and correct these immediately. It can help to look at the positive side of what at first displeases you:

- You may think he is too distant, remote, and unavailable. You could think that he doesn't know you yet.
- You may think he is better than you are and wish you were such a winner. You could think that this isn't a competition.
- You may think, "He is not good enough for me—who needs this loser?" You could think that the light is too dim in this bar to see his many good qualities, and besides, nobody is perfect.
- You may think he is not dressed the way you might like him to be. You could think that perhaps it's because he just came from a construction project, the minefields, or the gym.

Avery, a close friend, used to be a hypercritical person, but one day there was Walter, his houseguest, sitting at the breakfast bar waiting for Avery to serve him breakfast. Avery at first thought, "He is a lazy creep." Then, rethinking his first impression, he thought, "He is just relaxing after a hard week's work, and is probably in a coma from having too many drinks the night before." So Avery avoided the temptation to make a sarcastic remark like, "Who was your last slave?" or "Here comes breakfast, unclamp your umbilical cord." Instead, Avery decided to consider Walter a good man on the whole, though only half awake. That was twenty years ago, and they are doing fine as a couple today.

Demoralized and Despondent

Some love-averse behaviors are the product of having become too demoralized to go after what you want and ought to have. Perhaps you have bought into the negative things others have said about you. Now you feel too unworthy to look for someone to be close to, not special enough to believe the people who say they like you, and not entitled enough to be loved by anyone you might want. You become one of those men who, in conflict about their erotic desires, ashamed of wanting a lover, guilty about achieving any success at all in life, self-destructive due to internal and internalized homophobia, and fearful about letting loose in love, can only look longingly at people then look away, thinking the people you are looking at are incredulous at you for even daring to show some interest in them. Soon enough, pessimism about your chances of finding happiness becomes justified because, like anyone else who feels he doesn't deserve much, you ask for very little, and that is exactly what you get.

I think the best way to overcome demoralization is to force yourself to get moving just a bit, just enough to have that all-important minor initial success. That starts a virtuous cycle going. You start that climb out of your rut, then make day one of the climb the day where your depression becomes the worst day of the rest of your life. Try not to think that you will be hurt by, or lose, anyone you find. Don't leave him just to get there first, before he leaves you. Put thoughts like,

"He wouldn't want me," or "I am not good enough for him," or even, "He seems so great that there just has to be something wrong with him," out of your mind, at least for now. Don't fear the unknown as if it can only surprise you in a negative way. Remember that pessimistic predictions about what the future holds mostly come true because they are part of a secret plan to be unkind to, and hurt, yourself.

Try not to let early injuries rule your life. Try to get over the bad things your parents may have done to you, and get past an old relationship that turned sour on you. If you become convinced that because bad things have happened before they will necessarily happen again, your motto becomes, "Nothing ventured, nothing lost." Try not to fight old battles over and over again. New people won't necessarily treat you as badly as people did in the past. Besides, brooding about an abusive past, and provoking new abuse to reenact it, this time hopefully with a better outcome, doesn't help. It doesn't get rid of the hurt already inside, it just refreshes it. It's better to put the past behind you, see new people as different from the old ones, and learn how to trust again.

Certainly don't give up on sex. Gays as a group get a reputation for being too sexually oriented. The biggest secret of gay life is that many gay men aren't too sexually oriented, they are not sexually oriented enough. Shy and afraid of relationships, they focus away from men and onto substitute gratifications for having a man, ranging from old-movie nostalgia to a consuming interest in gay politics. Instead, keep your mind focused on developing relationships, and keep the nostalgia in the past—which is exactly where it belongs.

Self-homophobia

Self-homophobia arises for a number of reasons. It can come from swallowing others' hateful thoughts and feelings toward gays, or from guilt about being gay and having gay sexual fantasies. Whatever its origin, self-homophobia has both nonsexual and sexual manifestations. Nonsexual self-homophobia manifests behaviorally, especially in the realm of relationships. It might result in exaggerated gestures demanding the limelight, or in other forms of self-destructive time-wasting that focus away from the task of finding a partner. That can demoralize you, which can only lead to a sense of failure and more self-homophobia. I discuss the sexual aspects of self-homophobia in chapter 11, on solving sexual problems.

The best way to overcome self-homophobia is to understand where the homophobe is coming from. In my opinion, people who are homophobic toward gay men are suffering from an emotional illness. While homophobia has cultural roots, it is basically not much different from paranoia, depression, or antisocial personality disorder. For example, the homophobe with an antisocial personality disorder attacks a gay man or gays as a group simply to achieve some special personal goal, for example to win a political contest or get a job promotion. Viewing homophobia as an illness gives you a useful "them" not "us" perspective that can help you relax in the recognition that they, not you, are the one with the problem.

Understanding how homophobes achieve their negative effects helps too. Like a kid telling another kid who criticizes him, "You're one, too," they hurl accusations at gay men to deflect from their own difficulties and manifest faults. They mesmerize with their narcissism, acting like experts in morality even when their own morality is suspect, in religion even though they may have no formal affiliation, and in psychology even though they have little or no professional training.

Selecting the right counterstrike helps too. You can attack with your wits not with your fists, and say something and complain when you hear others making homophobic remarks. Ultimately, the best way to counteract homophobia is to not give it power over you. You must do everything in your power to love yourself and accept that being gay is just a part of who you are. Accentuate the positive aspects of yourself, such as your creativity, originality, and capacity for empathy. The latter technique has helped a number of my patients feel better *about* themselves, to the point that they started acting better *to* themselves.

Low Self-esteem

Many gay men who are demoralized are that way because they suffer from low self-esteem. Many single gay men say their self-esteem is low because they cannot find a lover. They think, "What is wrong with me if I cannot seem to find anyone?" In fact, the low self-esteem comes first, and creates the problem with finding (and keeping) a lover. First, you don't like yourself. As a result, other people tend to agree with you.

Earlier, I noted that the term "low self-esteem" refers to the self-dislike some gay men feel for themselves. They feel that they are no good at all and think that anyone who wants them must be desperate, pushy, just into sex, or suffering from a bout of bad judgment. I also mentioned that low self-esteem can be either appropriate or inappropriate. It is appropriate when it is the product of an awareness of, and so a reasonable response to, one's truly bad behavior and the consequences of that behavior, as in, "I really hurt him by walking out on him one day without warning and never coming back." It is inappropriate when it is exaggerated, often completely irrational, and based on an unrealistic self-evaluation that leads a person who is good, or good enough, to view himself as bad.

Inappropriate low self-esteem can be due to:
- Excessive guilt about your sexuality.
- Excessive guilt about your anger.
- Second thoughts about a high self-esteem you ultimately come to recognize is not entirely warranted.
- Self-blame from failing to realize ideals even when the ideals are too high ever to be met.
- Social factors, where a negative self-assessment is taken over, unchanged, from others' assessment of you.

Whether low self-esteem is appropriate or inappropriate, gay men whose self-esteem is low are at a big disadvantage when it comes to finding partners. Gay men who feel unworthy don't feel entitled to having a committed relationship. They don't find one either, in part because others tend to judge you based on how you judge yourself, an unfortunate example of how people usually get what they think they deserve. Or they accept someone unworthy of them because they think that is all they can get, or what they should have. Feeling depressed, they become too self-destructive to find someone for themselves. They make sure they remain alone as a way to punish themselves for assumed crimes and imagined sins. They blame themselves for doing forbidden sexual things, and live out their self-blame by staying home, or, if they go out, by being tentative and unresponsive in their relationships with others. They actually retreat or recoil when they see a nice man coming, doing so out of a fear that he might lead them into temptation. If this is you, other men don't know what you desire because you don't speak up about what you want. You may even confuse others by sending them mixed messages. Naturally, men like this get rejected. Then they feel they deserve it, and hesitate to try again. Should they be accepted, they feel that they don't deserve it, and either ignore it because it doesn't fit in with preconceived notions about themselves or do something to screw things up.

This vicious cycling can lead to pessimism, with a dark view of the world just waiting to be validated. In their teens or twenties, low self-esteem men think they are too young to be married; in their thirties and forties, they retreat to feeling too middle-aged to be desirable; and in their fifties and sixties, they back off because they see themselves as over the hill—too old for anyone to want them.

They bad-mouth themselves verbally in public and tear themselves down by the way they act. For example, they might wear a shabby schlemiel costume to drive home the point that they are big nobodies—an outfit that starts on top with a smart hair shirt and ends below in an alluring matching iron boot.

Morris, an old friend, just started at a new gym. Morris is an older man now, but his mother, whom he closely resembles, was still beautiful at eighty-five, and Morris still looks good too. Morris knows people in the gym and on the streets, some really good-looking men, are looking longingly at him, but he just cannot bring himself to believe it. He says to himself, "That cannot be, I am so old. If they are looking at me it must be because they are wondering why someone so old still goes to the gym; or they are hustlers; or they are foreigners from a culture that likes older American men because they are desperate to marry an American citizen; or they have dim vision." Morris conveys his attitude not as low self-esteem but as disinterest because he doesn't look back at the people who look at him.

Dealing with low self-esteem and demoralization is more complex than just raising it by dint of willpower or through psychotherapy. There is a range of solutions to this problem. Here are some steps you might take.

Distinguish Appropriate from Inappropriate Low Self-esteem

The first kind, appropriate low self-esteem, means you have to stop doing bad things to yourself (and to others). The second kind, inappropriate low self-esteem, means you have to start thinking better of yourself (and others).

Correct for Emotional Bias towards Yourself

Realize how often feelings of worthlessness are the product of a negative emotional bias towards yourself. Low self-esteem invariably involves distortion, exaggeration, and self-prejudice. Much of this self-prejudice results from the belief that being gay is an illness or morally wrong, when in reality it is just a fact of life.

Look for Endless Logical Loops That Keep You Thinking in a Box

One example of such an endless loop might be: people don't like you because you don't like yourself; you don't like yourself because people don't like you. Next, interrupt these loops by putting your foot down and judging yourself less harshly, and refusing to put yourself in a "can't-win" position.

Stay Away from Critical People

Stay away from people who aggravate your paranoia and depression, no matter how cute they are. If you can't because you are in a closed space with them, at least recognize that most critical people have their own agendas, and that every criticism of you is a self-criticism, one that underneath is really meant for themselves.

Minimize Your Use of Projection as a Way to Lift Your Self-esteem

Projection never solves self-esteem problems. At first you feel better after dealing with your own sense of failure by blaming other people for the things that go wrong in your life. Then you do nothing corrective, so the real failures continue exactly as before, and multiply.

Have Some Real Successes

Gay men who have real successes feel less like a failure and find their self-image improves as well. Give up searching for Mr. Far Right, and look for Mr. Middle of the Road. Don't choose someone unworthy of you, just be a little more modest about what you expect in a man, and out of life.

Don't Sell Short What You Get

Don't, at the moment of truth, think that if it's yours then by definition it cannot be any good—the Groucho Marx mentality, where you ask yourself, "How worthwhile could he be if he is interested in joining me?"

Don't View Your Failures as Cumulative

Failures don't add up. What happened in the past doesn't count. Life is like a series of throws of the dice. The next throw doesn't know a thing about the last one.

Don't Ever Put Yourself Down in Public

Avoid self-demeaning humor because that only makes other people ask themselves, "What does he know about himself that I don't know?" Self-deprecating jokes, about being gay, about being Jewish, or the like, demean who and what you are. Also avoid self-demeaning behavior, particularly low self-esteem lived out in appearance foibles, like ineffectual hair combovers or hair transplants, or plastic surgery that is bad because you didn't hire the right surgeon. Right from the start, even before you have resolved your problem of low self-esteem, control your tendency to display it. Displaying it can lead to more of the same, because you become socially isolated, then you blame and dislike yourself for being a loner.

Don't Compare Yourself to Others

Evaluate yourself as an individual. Invidious comparisons with others, gay and straight, where you equate "I am different from," with "I am worse than," are often an important part of the distortive process.

Do a Complete Self-evaluation

When evaluating yourself, take all of your characteristics into account, not just your worst ones. If you must compare yourself with someone else, at least don't compare your looks to his without also comparing your personalities. Be all that you are, not just one or two of your worst characteristics.

Enumerate Your Good Points to Yourself

Do that over and over again. Remember that what you think of as your poison is another man's meat. Albert's lover threw him over for being too passive. Ian picked him up immediately because passive men were exactly what he liked.

Do Not Try to Overcompensate

Props like a beautiful apartment or a summer home don't help you lift your self-esteem in any meaningful way. These are OK to have, but only for themselves, not to impress someone and try to get them to love you.

Feeling that you are making yourself attractive, you might be tempted to brag to someone you just met about what a wonderful job or duplex you have. People know that you are trying to overcompensate, and say to themselves, "If he is so unself-assured, then there may be something wrong with him, something he knows about himself that I don't know." Besides, showing off this way can backfire. Emphasizing the things you have inspires envy and jealousy, and people leave you to get back at you for having more than they have. Donald used to brag about his two-bedroom New York apartment, but these days, with apartments being so difficult to come by in the city, he doesn't say anything because people just hate him for his good fortune and for having something they don't. Also these things are yours—and you are more likely to keep them than to share them. Who really wants to live in an apartment where everything belongs to you?

Francis, a friend, stopped bragging about all he had after he discovered the futility of doing so the hard way. When he reached a certain age, he wanted to be liked not for what he was and what he did, but for what he had. He talked constantly of his decorating triumphs in his centrally located apartment with the fabulous view. Mark, meeting Francis, told him, in effect, "I won't marry you because if I do I will spend the rest of my life caressing the wallboard."

Accept Your Specialness

Instead of trying to change yourself completely for someone, try to find someone who finds you attractive pretty much as you are. Instead of just accepting your own and others' negativity and attempting to change in significant ways, make yourself the best possible version of you. While you might need some work, basically you, like most people, are likely to be good enough already. If you are an older man, don't try to fool people into thinking you are younger, or to sway people who just don't like older people. Some aging gay men go to extremes to make themselves look younger and presumably more alluring, only to overhear people saying, "Why doesn't he just get it over with and put the other foot in the grave." Instead of trying to hide your age, make it part of your appeal. If life has made you an overripe fruit, act like a delicious preserve.

Compensate for Any Real Major Shortcomings You Might Possess

If you don't have looks, youth, money, and major pecs, work on what you can have, like a nice and welcoming personality.

Be as accomplished physically as you can be. It never hurts to eat a healthy diet to maintain your weight, go to the gym, and give up smoking and heavy drinking for health reasons, and because you will look much better too. Also, be as accomplished professionally as you can be. Next to being loving, being accomplished professionally is the greatest self-starter, and aphrodisiac, of them all. It gives any potential lover a feeling of achievement (by osmosis), and a sense of shared (adopted) pride. Make a good living so that you can be a "DINK"—someone who contributes to the comfortable living possible when two salaries are combined. (Having money is especially important when there are age differences.)

Become Your Own Best Self-promoter

Overcompensate, in a healthy way, by talking yourself up, always remembering that much of what people think about you is based on what you think about yourself. However, avoid swinging into denial where you think you are great as things stand, so that you do not to have to make some necessary repairs.

Develop a Positive Regard for Others

Follow this golden rule: if you don't have something good to say about someone, don't say anything at all. Although they might not show it, many gay men you meet are as down on themselves, and depressed too, as you are. Love them and they will thank you from the bottom of their hearts, which is where their love for you will be coming from.

In conclusion, what is the right attitude to maintain? Be a person who is neither too down on nor too stuck on himself. A matter-of-fact attitude toward yourself, where you view yourself as good, but not better or best, is nice too. Feel worthy of success and unworthy of punishment. You wouldn't mind having someone perfectly right or even wonderful but you look for someone OK, if imperfect, and you don't seek out or accept losers because you think that is what you deserve. Your self-despair and guilt is at a minimum, and you recognize that being gay is no big deal, so you don't walk around with a hang-dog look or scream about how wonderful life is just to convince yourself that it isn't as terrible as you fear. Be friendly and warm, seek people out without being too pushy, and never snub people or lead them on just to be able to turn them off because doing so makes you feel better about yourself. Be neither an avowed pessimist who thinks that nothing good will ever happen to you nor a cockeyed optimist who believes that everything is wonderful just as things stand. Believe that good things will happen but don't expect them to come your way every night, so don't see it as a catastrophe when Saturday becomes Sunday without your having achieved all your goals for the week.

There you are, a picture of satisfaction and strength, just glowing softly, gently lighting his way across the room, to you.

An Action-Oriented Approach to Dealing with Love-Averse Behavior and Low Self-esteem

Here are some good ways to accept love and be more positive about yourself.

Be Positive When You Are Looking for Love

Suppress the urge to make "no" the first word out of your mouth. Instead, practice saying "maybe" whenever a "no" tempts. Look in the mirror. See how the word "no" pulls your face down into a frown? See how the word "maybe" pulls your facial muscles back into a smile?

Get Over Your Shyness

When you approach someone, or he approaches you, offer him a firm hand not a limp one, and try to avoid blushing. Look, even stare, at people around you. Some men will get uncomfortable, other men will get interested.

Be Available to Others Who Are Looking for Love

Try not to surround yourself with friends who form an impregnable shield and an impenetrable wall against anyone who might want to get to you, driving others off as if they were rescuing you from an assailant. Heavy candlelight dinners with friends make you look unavailable to that interesting man at the next table and keep you from noticing that out there someone is trying to break through the firewalls you have erected around yourself.

Deal with Your Anxiety

If your cruising anxiety is really severe, try to avoid concentrated cruising where you set aside times when you are open for business and times when you are closed to opportunity. For you, low-key, constant cruising is a much better idea. Take safe baby steps instead of dangerous giant steps, and get where you are going with fewer disruptions by taking the long, local way around. Don't just settle for the road less traveled. Go Robert Frost one better and take the slow, easy cow path. Here you won't be intimidated by much, if any, traffic, and can avoid the emotional roadblocks and the white-knuckle anxiety that go with figuratively being on the busy highway.

For you, networking is a particularly good idea because it involves slowly building an ever-widening circle of contacts that may safely and comfortably lead you to the big contact of them all. With networking, you get where you are going without feeling rushed, experiencing demoralizing anxiety or depression, or being ruined by the hopeless feeling that every night without a contact is a night wasted, and your life is over because you didn't meet a lover last Saturday. Successful networkers remember that some Saturdays are better than others. Perhaps you caught someone's eye and inserted yourself into his mind for future consideration. Successful networkers remind themselves that love stories usually take three hundred pages to unfold, typically move forward only in the face of obstacles, and that only in tragedies do people meet and marry on page one. Successful networkers, to paraphrase an old aphorism, want him for good, not for Tuesday. Get introduced around and meet more and more people until you find your lover. Accept that it can take weeks to months, or even years, but that's better than foolishly rushing around then having to retreat afterwards.

Networking had a happy ending for Joe, a friend, who was seriously anxious about relationships. The person he met one night introduced him to a friend who introduced him to his lover who introduced him to a friend who introduced him to his lover who introduced him to his friend who was to become Joe's current, permanent lover. This process was leisurely enough for Joe to be able to tolerate. It took thirty years, but it was worth the wait.

Give Up a Little Independence to Connect

Some men haven't come to terms with their dependency. These gay men fear dating because to them it means that they will meet someone and become overly dependent on him. I suggest making friends with that fear by trying to relax, accepting your positive feelings about Mr. Wonderful, and thinking twice about seeing people who want you as intimidating, controlling, or voracious. A reassuring thought for you to have (but a bad philosophy for you, or anyone else, to live by) is that, being gay, you can, almost anytime you choose, get out of a deep and lasting relationship, and without even a moment's notice.

Get Over Some Dependency So That You Can Connect

If you fear cruising not because it will make you dependent but because it will interfere with one or more dependent relationships you already have, try to be a bit less close to your family and friends. Many gay men fear that if they find a lover they will not gain a husband but lose a mother. They stay lonely for the rest of their lives just to avoid the possibility that if they strike out on their own they might antagonize their parents and not find someone to replace them either. If you are too close to Mom and Dad, start breaking away, at least a little, now. Invite friends over to your place for the holidays and spend some holiday time with them. As long as you are independent and emancipated (that is, you are over a certain age and no longer your parent's responsibility), stay at his house overnight instead of coming home. Just call to tell your parents where you are and that you are safe. Yes, you might have to leave home if you fall in love. Mom might retaliate and Dad might clutch his chest. But that's their problem, and a chance you will just have to take.

Try to make your own choices in a man too. Don't pick the men your parents, or friends, pick for you, if he's not what you want. Don't give up on the whole idea of a committed relationship just to please a mother who really doesn't want you to be gay, or want you to leave home, or want you to love anyone but her.

Another good idea is to deal with your dependency by turning the tables and letting others be dependent on you. Reciprocate invitations and treat even the most generous people you know to a drink or a dinner whenever you can afford it. It will make them feel comfortable with you, and give you vicarious satisfaction as well.

Get Over Your Fear of Trusting Other Men

Try to develop as much basic trust as you can. It is the most important element in connecting to commit. Be a little less wary than you are now, while still watching it with people who are dangerous. It is certainly unwise to hitchhike in the hills and get picked up by someone in a rusted pickup truck with a black Labrador retriever in the back that goes nicely with that shiny gun in the glove compartment. But somewhere along the line you have to avoid going to the opposite extreme, and trust someone enough to get intimate with him.

Elliott, a fearful patient, would never take someone home with him. Instead, he would always insist on going to their place, no matter how well he knew them. Making a joke out of it, he said, "That way, in case I am murdered, my blood will be on their carpet," and, "Mainly I feel safer in their place than in mine because I know how hard it is to get rid of a body." Later in life he did start taking people home, but only after he knew them for a few months or more, and out of caution put a lock on his inside door and locked it after entering so that they couldn't get out unless Elliott were still alive enough to open the door for them. We worked together to have Elliott apply the rules of evidence. Check someone out in real time. Ask around if anyone knows the person you are interested in. Better still, meet a new man in a public place the first few times before going home with him. Get his phone number, call him back, and even call him at work if he lets you.

Don't Blank Out at the Moment of Truth

Try not to blank out when good things start happening, floating off defensively when someone approaches and tries to get close to you. If you are the type who flinches and backs off when something great appears on the horizon, sensitize yourself to recognizing the problem and practice focusing, which means saying "yes" and "OK" whenever a good opportunity comes your way. Joe, a friend, once told me that he was at the record store looking for a certain opera when the man next to him started bothering him, trying to make conversation. It was as if Joe automatically shrunk from anything that looked like a violet. He needed to erect firewalls between himself and others. Of course, after the man got away he kicked himself, asking himself, too late, "What was I thinking of at the time, anyway?"

Enjoy Your Life

It is hard enough to avoid having the bad luck of the draw without also having the draw of the bad luck, so try to put the whole idea of getting pleasure from suffering out of your mind. There is very little to be gained from torturing yourself by going to the right places and doing things wrong when you get there, becoming restless before the night is done, and panicking and leaving early just when you think that good things are about to happen to you.

Don't Compensate Too Much

Compensating looks like just the opposite of demoralization, but it is really little more than the flip side of the same coin. It takes the form of flamboyant franticness, where you overuse two of the most overused of gay words, "fantastic" and "fabulous." You live by them, enjoying your life not too little but too much. You reason according to the formula, "I am not unworthy of you, I am too good for you," and become the life of the party, scattering lots of confetti just to hide the fact that no one has invited you to the ball. Instead of feeling you deserve nothing and no one, you think you are too good for ordinary mortals, and refuse to talk to strangers, in particular those sluts who deign to talk to you.

When it comes to connecting, it sounds as though it is better to like than to hate yourself too much, but it isn't. It doesn't really matter if you feel unworthy of someone or you feel someone is unworthy of you, whether you hear him knocking and assume it isn't for you, or you hear him knocking but are too imperious and grand, too tasteful or aristocratic, to come to the door and just answer it.

Try not to become:

- superficial to the point that others don't take you seriously;
- stuck-up, so that others think they aren't good enough for, and don't have a chance with, you;
- self-preoccupied, talking about yourself all the time, which makes others feel left out, and as if they don't count;
- dominant, which leaves others feeling uncomfortably submissive;
- selfish and self-centered, which gives others the feeling that all you want is something from them;
- aggressive, pushing too hard to get what you feel you deserve, even when it's at others' expense; or
- overly fussy, and critical of others, goofing on them, making them feel inadequate, and discarding them.

Don't Drink Too Much

Suppress the urge to overuse drugs and alcohol. It's hard to connect when you pass out, and it's hard to connect tonight if you feel guilty the morning after about how you behaved the night before. My patients told me that the best times of their lives were when they completely gave up alcohol, pills, and smoking. They felt better, looked better, and really enjoyed their new sobriety. My personal experience with intoxicants tells me they were right on the money.

Deal with Promiscuity

Believe it or not, promiscuous men can fear cruising too. They just deal with their fears by denying them and going to the opposite extreme. If you are currently promiscuous, think about first getting it out of your system, then becoming less promiscuous. Otherwise, your promiscuity tends to feed on itself, as the more sex you have, the more sex you want.

Try looking within to understand why you feel you must be promiscuous. Start by asking yourself the following questions:

- Do I want multiple partners or is something inside of me forcing me to have them?
- Am I enjoying myself or am I being driven to act, without much pleasure, by something deep within?
- Do I hate being promiscuous but find myself unable to stop?
- Am I rationalizing my promiscuity as a good thing so that I can avoid feeling like a bad person?
- Is my promiscuity a ritual, that is, am I having sex in an attempt to solve a personal problem in sexual terms? For example, am I proving my desirability and worth by impressing others with the number of conquests I have had? Are my conquests the stuff for bragging to friends about how many I had last night?
- Is my promiscuity a compensation for low self-esteem, a way to feel aristocratic by distinguishing myself, at least as I see things, from the common *hausfrau*, you know the kind, the dull boy who, like the silly goose, can do no better than to mate for life?
- Am I overcompensating for being sad by forcing myself to be happy all the time?
- Am I overcompensating for being lonely by never being alone again, even for a minute?
- Am I trying to avoid stagnation in order to convince myself that I am alive and well and won't die?
- Is mine a revenge promiscuity where I am being promiscuous to spite a specific person in my life, perhaps my parents (after all your parents wouldn't want you to be promiscuous, would they?) or an old or present lover? Am

I am screwing around in a way that assures that he finds out about it and suffers accordingly, just as I planned all along?

- Am I just trying to keep up with the Joneses? Am I envious of what they have and competing to get it so that I can have more than they do?
- Does my promiscuity stand for my independence? For example, am I proving how little I need the "sisters" I no longer have, having in my promiscuity offended them by slipping away, in stealth, with their husbands?
- Am I a neophiliac, that is, do I need to have something new at all times, with mine a need to undress everything I see?
- Is peer pressure an important reason for my becoming promiscuous?

Peer pressure to be promiscuous is very strong in gay circles, and most gay men's attitude about promiscuity is influenced by current thinking in the gay community. Some in the gay community currently devalue monogamous relationships. "Creative promiscuity," which is a way of saying that there are methods available to avoid AIDS, has set the tone of many of today's discussions. Though promiscuity is a way to keep up your standing in a gay community that values sexual freedom, that doesn't make it right for you. It just means that you will be joining a certain segment of the gay community that likes to use the logic of the clever fox explaining why it should be allowed to guard the hen house. These men come up with one reason after another why it is okay to separate sex from commitment, all amounting to rationalizations for screwing around guilt-free. Notably, they don't come up with the most important reason of all for doing just the opposite: there are better ways to find Mr. Delicious than subjecting every man in the world to a taste test.

Here's some advice. When you meet Mr. Right think, "I want you. I want you completely. I don't want you to have someone else. I want you to be faithful to me. I will be faithful to you." Then act like you mean it. Right from the start, avoid making alternative arrangements such as, "One night stands only, because anything more permanent makes sex look like love." Learn to live with temptation, and be willing to sanctify any budding relationship by being religiously faithful to it. Don't get into the bad habit of attempting to improve your sex life by thinking of having sex with someone else while you are doing it with someone, autoconditioning your mind to wander. You can, of course, increase your sexual pleasure with your present partner by running that feather over his whole body, or spraying him with whipped cream (low-fat, of course) and licking it off. Better still, make that unnecessary by harnessing the capacity you already have inside you for exquisite sexual pleasure with the man you love. You won't need aids and props if you just remove obstacles to feeling and expressing the joy that's already there, obstacles like guilt, a fear of commitment, and a poor self-image that make it difficult for you to give yourself a vote of confidence, and tell the sex police to shut up.

In conclusion, I advocate understanding promiscuity, not condemning it. I advocate viewing it as a central part of the distancing process that can adversely affect your relationships. Others notice that you are too sexually frantic to connect and too busy to settle down. That's just one reason why promiscuity is the best illustration of all of how good sex can be the single biggest enemy of great relationships.

I personally think you should target your life to finding a lover with whom to build and maintain a committed, monogamous relationship. Certain variations are acceptable too, but I prefer the theme itself, and in spite of the general trend to accept other lifestyles as equally viable, I see these as compromises, not as intriguing modifications.

Distractions

Some gay men looking for a lover tend to start off on the right foot, then head in the wrong direction. They get involved in things that make them feel temporarily better but actually divert them from their primary goal. Relationships take work, work means being focused, and being focused means avoiding distractions.

Avoid Substitute Gratifications

It's so easy to plug substitute gratifications into your life to make yourself feel better about not having what you should, and could, have. These include activities that are neither corrective nor reparative. Any pleasurable activities done by your-self or with friends may qualify, including high-gear cruising, screaming yourself into an artificial euphoria, and having a big email buddy list that enables you to exchange double-entendres with the speed, but not the luminosity, of light.

Eschew Wild Sex

My advice is to give up sex clubs, the baths, phone sex, and reading and answer-ing the personal ads for sex. Just imagine: would Mozart have ever gone as far as he did if when he was a child he refused to knuckle down to work because he insisted on having fun making obscene phone calls and charging them to his father Leopold's credit card?

Love Your Pet but Not to Distraction

Dogs are substitute gratifications that give you the feeling that you have compan-ionship, which takes the edge off your need to meet someone. On a practical level, they also keep you from doing some of the things that you have to do to meet peo-ple, as in, "No I cannot go there or do that, because my dog needs me at home." Ellis actually announced that he was married to his dog. That's not a good sign.

Volunteer Just the Right Amount

Volunteering is good. Too much of a good thing can, however, distract you from your goals. Doing charitable work when you feel needy yourself can make you feel even needier. That can be very depressing. At this stage of your life, it is par-ticularly important to avoid being excessively concerned with others. An intense focus on and identification with social responsibilities, one that many gay men engage in, is admirable, but it can be overly self-sacrificial.

Keep Busy but not Nonproductively

Often, people will tell lonely gay men to keep busy in order to deal with being alone. I have also suggested that, and it's good advice as far as it goes. But it shouldn't go too far and distract you from accomplishing a specific goal: being less alone. It is certainly not OK to keep busy if you are doing one thing to avoid doing another thing that you should be doing. Wielding the glue gun to make delightful cachepots out of empty oatmeal boxes is not OK if it becomes an end in and of itself. And besides, as a single man, what are you going to do with all those cachepots, living as you do in a skillfully decorated single-room occupancy? Be especially on the lookout for too many "make work" activities. These can throw you into overdrive. Leave some time to quietly reflect on how you got where you are and how to get out of it. Look for some meaningful ways to structure your life so that you can feel full enough to last until your next meal.

One example of useful busy-ness comes from my own experience, and involves my favorite panacea: exercise in the gym, something I stress more than once in this book. I was alone in a big country house and I was just too lonely to stay there for more than a few hours, until I filled time and broke up the day by exercising. I remember my words to this day: "I don't have any trouble on Sunday mornings now that I exercise from 10–12 A.M." I calmed down and really began to enjoy the country, even though at the time I was there for long stretches by myself. And I began to look better too, which helped my chances a lot.

Accept All Invitations

Too many gay men miss opportunities to network by refusing to meet their straight married friends, or by insisting on leaving a straight party early because they want to get on with the gay cruising. Remembering the principles behind networking, make it a rule to say to yourself, "Anytime I am with someone, any-one, I am looking."

Don't Focus Too Much on Wanting to Leave Your Mark on the World

Some gay men, workaholics in particular, think that having a lover isn't as important as leaving a legacy behind when they die. They want to leave an entry in that great computer search engine of the cybersky, so that one thousand years from now when someone looks at the database of the most famous and successful men of the centuries, their name pops up in the Top 10 choices. Remind yourself of all the really popular people who are forgotten now. When is the last time you heard a song by Richard Rogers, or even Cole Porter? Recognize that unless you are Mozart, after you die others will never hear from or about you again. There is no place in relationships for monument building. When it comes to leaving marks, that hickey on your lover's neck will do just fine. Be happy now, instead of spending your whole life trying to be the most important person in the cemetery, and the envy of all the new kids on the plot.

Don't Become Too Preoccupied with Coming Out

Come out to yourself and put that behind you to avoid getting caught up in regrets about being gay to the detriment of being gay all the way. Suppress those hopeless feelings about being gay that spread to hopeless feelings about ever having any sort of life.

Coming out to yourself involves eliminating self-homophobia. Without self-homophobia, there will be little or no real reason to stay in with yourself. Be clear that being gay is not a liability, it is not an asset, it just is. It is simply a variant of normal, like being redheaded or left-handed. Give up feeling despair over being gay. It's irrational. True, there are certain things you cannot do as a gay man. For example, many gay men do not have children of their own. But there are ways to compensate for that. You can compensate for not having children by finding a lover and assuring his happy future, or even by adopting. Always remember too that you may not need to compensate for being childless. Having children is not entirely the unmixed blessing your romantic fantasies make it out to be. Consider the possibility that your wish to have children may really be a longing for what you cannot have, just another one of those things you want because you don't have it, and someone else does.

Coming out to others is optional. What you do in this realm depends on you, your personality, your circumstances, and most of all, how it might affect your search for a relationship, or a particular relationship you already have going. A preoccupation with strategies for coming out to others can sap energy that would otherwise be available for purposes of connecting. Coming out might hurt you professionally, and ruin your finances and professional status and other assets you have to offer a lover. If you have a special lover in mind, he might not be interested in your coming out, or he might even think your being out will hurt him, again personally or professionally. Besides, so often a preoccupation with coming out is telling him: important causes first, you next. Also, coming out is war, while relationships are surrender. Coming out to others is "good" practice for a confrontational approach that can make you generally too hostile for what should be your primary, loving purpose. Coming out is a noisy process. In contrast, love creeps in on tiptoe. Now get over it, and onto finding a man.

Put the Gay Political Scene in Perspective

Politics and relationships don't always mix. Richard, a hairdresser, was soon to discover the negative effects of his all-consuming interest in boycotting bars that didn't treat gay men in general, and him in particular, right. He had become all involved in boycotting a bar whose owner insulted him and his friends. That left very little time for what should have been his primary pursuit, finding a man and treating him well. His boycotting the bars barred him from meeting the boys. Richard also spent too much time approaching people on the street, not to get to meet them but to get them to sign his various petitions about noise pollution, tenants rights, and defeating high-rise construction projects likely to block his view. Because he was a very personable chap, others' faces lit up when he approached. But the light in their faces was his cue to tell them that he wasn't interested in them, he just wanted their name, address, and phone number so that their signatures on his petition would be valid.

An Action Plan for Dealing with Distractions

While distractions might offer temporary relief from tension, go without them so that pressure builds until you cannot stand it any longer, and simply have to make some real changes. Accept that without pain there is no gain. Cut off at least some of your supply of comforts so that you can get leaner and hungrier by the day until you just have to do something to ease your discomfort. Then don't slip back into the luxury of immediate gratification. Instead, continue to postpone immediate gratification for the rewards of reaching long-term goals.

Now that you have overcome your fear of commitment and inertia, gotten through being lonely without having it hold you back unduly or creating permanent problems for yourself, accepted your native desire and ability to love, and have stayed the course by staying the cruise without riding your boat up on a sandbar, you are ready for the next chapter, dealing with special concerns.

10

Special Concerns and Considerations

In chapter 9, you learned all about obstacles to success and how to overcome them. In chapter 10, I go into special situations: some ways to be available and attractive when you are older; solving sexual problems; and seeking further help if needed. This chapter is appropriate for most gay men—even those who are young, potent, and functioning well, for it contains ideas that transcend their specific context to be universally applicable in all, or almost all, situations. So don't pass it by just because you at first don't think they apply to you.

Dealing with Getting Older

Getting older is a special problem for gay men who are still single later in life, who came out at an advanced age, or who lost a lover after being together for many years. These gay men often ask me, "Is it possible for an older man to find love?" I answer, "Yes, it is," and discuss how, if this is you, you can do it. Folklore says your situation is difficult to hopeless, but it isn't. Just look around you. Everyday observation says that you can meet someone nice whatever your age. It is done all the time.

What is "older" anyway? I define older as somewhere between first and last opportunity—anywhere, that is, from 18 to 105. If you are in my category of "older" and having problems meeting someone, ask yourself another question, my usual question, "Is there anything that, as an older man, I am doing, or not doing, to make it difficult to impossible for me to find love?" Your answers may surprise you. They will not necessarily be age related. Rather, they will probably be the same ones that applied when you were young. You will discover the same hesitance, the same pessimism, and the same problems with tactics that kept good things from happening to you when you were just starting out.

Here are some ways gay men can handle getting older in a positive way. Some of these techniques, suitably modified, are also applicable to handling all the bigotries besides ageism that affect gay, as well as straight, men.

No Shame

Never be ashamed of, or try to apologize for, your age. Instead, view yourself as special, no matter what your age. As is true of anything special, some people like it and others don't, so try to find someone who likes you, and who sees all the positive things you have to offer, without thinking much about every single little specific. Recognize that you can still be a valuable commodity when you are older, and that there are even advantages to having a relationship with an older man, who often makes a better partner than a younger man. For one thing, some personality problems improve with age, making older men positive, mature, interested in other people, mellow, less brash, more reliable, and more available. Older men are often more willing to make a relationship work than are their younger counterparts. They feel that it is too late to look for someone new, and, having already gotten the sex scene out of their system, never want to get back to the late hours, frantic cruising, and bruised egos again.

No Desperation

Avoid feeling desperate. That can only lead to taking desperate measures, and creating desperate situations. Matt, a patient, lost a lover to cancer when Matt was forty years old. Matt felt that a man his age was too old to meet someone new. People approached him but he felt they were just after his money, so he didn't respond to them. We discovered that Matt's real problem wasn't age related at all. It was that because he had never trusted in himself, he always believed that others felt as negatively about him as he felt about himself. Matt had irrational feelings of being too old when he was thirty. Being forty just gave him new and different reasons to feel that way.

As Matt became more and more pessimistic about the future, he began to act desperately, and foolishly, dying his hair too black and weaving one strand over his bald head in a futile attempt not to look as if his hair were thinning. He spent entirely too much time in the gym developing more muscles than he absolutely needed or that looked good on him.

Starting at age forty-one, Matt had a succession of flings. When Cal, the last one, left him it all began to seem hopeless to Matt and he became frantic, hitting the pornographic bookstores, the bushes, and the baths, desperately seeking anyone he could find to replace what he had lost.

One day his luck began to change. Cal's best friend looked Matt up and the two of them started going together. At first Matt, still reeling from Cal's loss, couldn't even think about loving again. Soon, however, the young man's steadfastness and obvious admiration and love for Matt won him over, and the two of them decided to commit to one another. They are still together today two decades later. Both are very happy with the arrangement and their age differences don't matter much, especially now that they have started to look, and act, like one another.

I once had a patient who tried aggressively to hide his age with a toupee, face lift, girdle, elevator shoes, and other subterfuges. This gentleman was good enough before his various transformations. All that these endeavors accomplished was to make him less desirable. This happened in part because he made people anxious, for he was facing them with their own mortality, the inevitability of future decay, the hopeless feeling that they couldn't do anything definitive about their status, and the certainty that anything they did about it would only make them look ridiculous. They dealt with that by dismissing him from their world. I helped him understand that many people might pass him by, not because he was older, but because he was strange, and there is something inherently self-defeating about that. Then we worked on improving both his appearance and his behavior. First I got him to lose some weight. I got him to remove the various appurtenances and to let his hair grow out naturally gray and cut it short and neat around the sides and back. When we were finished he looked like an older, thin, balding man who was not bad-looking for his age, although it was obvious that he had never been, and was never going to be, *l'homme fatale*. I also got him to stop camping up a storm, being the duenna of the dunes everywhere he went, and helped him at least play the part of a quiet, thoughtful, sophisticated, not particularly high-profile ordinary citizen.

That is exactly when he got noticed. The attention and accolades he always desired never came his way when he was all gussied up with no place to go. Now, with his new look, John, a middle-aged man who was tired of running around, wanted to settle down, and thought that my patient would be the perfect companion and sexual partner for him, took notice. John could never have loved Mr. Spare Parts. But Mr. Made Whole Again was exactly right for him.

Brett, a personal acquaintance and a much older man, had the right positive attitude about his age from the start. Brett, who was on the board of a New York cooperative, was in the hospital with pneumonia. After a few weeks in the hospital, he got a letter from the president of the board. He thought, "Good, he is sending me a get-well card." But alas not, for the letter said, "In view of your deteriorating health, I feel you should resign from the board." Brett refused to be intimidated. His reply was, "I sent him a letter back that told him I am not going anywhere." Brett let the board president, and everyone else as well, know that he felt he was OK as things stood. He knew that having a positive regard for yourself made a positive reaction to him more likely. He knew that when you like yourself, others tend to agree.

In his love life, Brett worked those truths for all they were worth, and another one too: "Don't look up to gorgeous young men as gods. Instead act like the god you are, stand back, and let them look up to, and worship, you." The last time I saw Brett he was hobbling along, supported by a nice-enough appearing younger man, someone who was seeking a fatherly person to take care of him, and wanted someone to take care of as well.

Live in the Present

Avoid dwelling on how wonderful things used to be before you were born or when you were very young. That only detracts from how wonderful things are, or could be, now. Besides, the past probably wasn't so great anyway. It was full of those people who thought the world was flat, the earth was at the center of the universe, and hadn't yet thought of, or refused to buy into, the germ theory of disease.

Address Your Own Ageism

If you are alone, expand your horizons by working to master your own negative attitudes toward people you deem to be too old. Morrie, an older gay man I treated, at first refused to go to a senior citizen's center because he felt there were only losers there. After all, these people let themselves get "disgustingly" old without doing something about it, didn't they? But with therapy, his attitude changed and he began to like the place, and he met someone there about his own age, too.

Strengthen Yourself

Make yourself as strong as possible. It's always a good idea to have adequate health and disability insurance. The latter protects you in case you cannot work. Check with a financial advisor or an insurance agent you trust. See a physician regularly, particularly one who understands the needs of gay men, and older gay men especially. Don't retire unless you have a lover who is retiring with you. Work as long as you can and if you lose, or retire from, your present job, shift over into another line of work, one that you as an older man can continue to do indefinitely. Don't hang around the house interfering with a partner's schedule by demanding he take time off from work to be, and do things, with you. Don't stagnate. Allan, an old friend, sits in his trailer all day with a laptop computer actually on his lap sending his few remaining friends off-color jokes and reprints of newspaper articles. He is interested, it seems, in nothing but sex. Sean, in contrast, became a late bloomer who started writing magazine articles on travel for a living, and is now much in demand with younger people who "just adore" being with, being seen with, and being written about by him.

If you do lose a lover when you are older, don't stay lonely until you go to your grave. Instead, unless you are close to going there when he goes, and you have adjoining cemetery plots, try to find someone else. If he really loved you, he will continue to understand.

Of course, older men can have all the problems and potentially use all the solutions I present in the rest of this book. I just don't view getting older as being so special that it puts you in a different category from other men. Thinking it does is the problem, and the solution is to keep looking for love in a common-sense way without having decided that you are too old to be able to follow the rules, or to follow them productively. Pessimism, low self-esteem, and compensatory grandiosity are common in middle-age men, but not any more so than they are in younger men. Just because you have reached a special age doesn't mean that coping with life and succeeding in love is that different from coping and succeeding when you are just starting out.

Solving Sexual Problems

This section describes how to resolve a number of sexual problems ranging from disinterest in and boredom with sex to impotence. If you don't have sexual problems you have one of two choices: you can skip this section, or you can read it for the basic information it contains about relationships and to learn about problems that a current or future partner may face. I think you should do the latter, because all of us flirt with some of the interpersonal problems described here that under other circumstances can become impediments to performing not only socially but sexually as well. Plus, it is always good to be aware of any problems you and your partner might face in the future.

Solving sexual problems is particularly important for gay men looking for Mr. Right when the sexual problems don't stop in the bedroom, but instead spill over into the personality, causing them to be shy about meeting new people. Now you have two problems: you can't have sex, and if you could, you wouldn't have anybody to have it with.

Solving sexual problems starts with identifying them. They aren't always easy to spot with any degree of certainty. Sometimes, deciding if you actually have a sexual problem is best left up to the professionals. Not everyone who thinks he has a sexual problem actually has one. Sex is never picture perfect, and one night's failure does not necessarily mean that something is basically wrong. Too many lovers see problems with one sex act as a cause for alarm, when the reality is that a sexual relationship takes time to develop. It often takes time to feel comfortable with someone new, so before you conclude that you have a sexual problem with a new lover, allow time to get used to him, to learn what he wants, and to get what you want through to him.

True sexual problems tend to occur regularly, not occasionally. They occur with many if not all partners, and are accompanied by a sense of performance disappointment and feelings of failure. Solving true sexual problems requires deep self-evaluation, and you might even have to seek medical or psychological help or visit a sex therapist. You may need help if you have:

- A complete inability to relax the anal sphincter during passive anal sex even after adequate foreplay, the gay male equivalent of *dyspareunia* (difficult or painful coitus in women).
- Certain forms of impotence, like a pervasive inability to get and keep an erection.
- *Ejaculatio tarda* (a condition where you can't come, no matter how hard you try).
- A preference for selfish paraphilias (paraphilia is the newer, and not necessarily better, word for perversion) such as rubbing to your orgasm without caring about satisfying him.

However, when ineptness, diffidence, lack of knowledge, and poor skill sets are the problem, simple solutions, such as those I propose in this chapter, can be the solution.

Making Sure You Are Doing It Right

Understand that sex takes work. You have to concentrate on what you are doing. You have to move, not just lie there, and you have to keep your interest from wandering. Neither of you can perform optimally if you are thinking of what you could be doing with someone else if only you weren't stuck there doing it with him.

Checking for Physical Incompatibility

Sometimes it is difficult to get a big peg into a small hole, or for a small peg to adequately fill a big hole. In extreme cases, the best that can be expected is a relationship without much in the way of sex, but that's OK too. One of the most touching love stories I know is of two patients of mine—who everyone called, because of the distinct resemblance, "Tweedle Dum and Tweedle Dee." These were two disabled gay veterans, both of whom were troubled emotionally. They tried sex but it rarely worked. But they didn't care, because they were in love with each other and they felt that the companionship was the most important thing and all they really needed.

Identifying the Specific Kind of Sexual Problem You Have

Sex is a normal function. However, there are varying degrees of normal. Everyone has a few problems like the ones I describe. The following problems have to be pretty severe and repetitive to cause concern and require special intervention.

Fear of Sex

Some gay men who are celibate, or close to it, prefer not to have sex. They are proud, perhaps inordinately, of how little they do it, how rarely it works when they try, and how it is not all it is cracked up to be when they succeed. Others don't want to be celibate—but they nevertheless find themselves shying away from sex. In effect, they are reassuring mother, "I don't touch myself down there, or if I do I don't enjoy it," and telling their partners, "And you shouldn't either." Guilt is often the problem and the solution is to give up the guilt, not the sex. Later in this chapter I suggest some ways to dispel guilt about sex. For starters, think constancy. Once you have found him, never let it go.

Boredom

Boredom with one's sexual partner leads to disinterest that frustrates the development of a new relationship and sends all concerned off looking for something better, when what they already have is good enough.

Boredom often takes the form of sex without pleasure. You act reluctant. You move slowly and in protest though you finally yield, perhaps with the wrong kind of audible sigh. Or you are completely dead in bed. Neither of you thinks the sex or the relationship worth pursuing because you believe there is no magic, or that the magic has gone out of it.

Boredom with sex is not inherent in gay relationships, new or old. When I hear, "The magic has gone out of my relationship," I think that in fact while magic is still possible, it is not being performed. Overfamiliarity is often cited as the culprit, but with good relationships sex gets less, not more, boring. When a relationship is solid, lust, although not necessarily in its original form, actually increases over the days, months, and years. In simple behavioral terms, having your cake makes you want another slice.

Boredom is, rather, an active process. The flame hasn't flickered and died, you just haven't given it adequate fuel. Instead of convincing yourself that "lust doesn't last," as if this happens passively, say to yourself, "I won't let lust lapse or lose its luster." Actively, purposefully, and deliberately make up your mind to enjoy your present company. You will discover that in a virtuous cycle joy leads to success, which leads to joy.

Impotence

Gay men who suffer from impotence cannot get or keep an erection, are partially anesthetic, or cannot have an orgasm, at least in a reasonable period of time, and may have to masturbate themselves (with or without a partner) to orgasm, often because of an intrusive thought, like, "I will never be able to come." They often suffer from failure panic, which makes it even harder to be successful. Personality problems compound the sexual problem as one feeds the other until the same problem occurs both supine and upright, with the limp phallus having become a paradigm for the limp relationship. The cure depends both on overcoming such personal fears as fear of commitment and passivity and on improving your performance directly. A partner's patience and encouragement can be a great deal of help, too, especially if he uses reverse psychology on you. He doesn't push you, you aren't scared, and fear and anxiety don't take over and constrict those blood vessels just when you need them to dilate.

Promiscuity and Cheating on a Lover

Promiscuity and cheating can be sexual problems, not nice little touches that add spice to the stew, or, at the very least, don't spoil the broth. The best way to deal with promiscuity is to ask yourself if you are having more sex than you really want and need. If you answer in the affirmative, cut down on the sex without making excuses for why it's not yet time to give up adolescent experimentation, a quest for variety, or your need to eat, drink, and be merry today for tomorrow you die.

Learning How to Do It

Ignorance is still possible these days, and is a common reason for sexual difficulties. Sometimes, even the most sophisticated gay men don't know some of the tricks. It's here that books like *The Joy of Gay Sex* come in handy.

However, some gay men who claim they don't know what to do sexually really do. They are just too guilty to admit they know it to themselves. Such terms as "Bad," "Dirty," and "NBC" ("Not Biblically Correct") fly through their minds.

Under such circumstances, reading books like the *Joy of Gay Sex* doesn't help that much. If you are one of these men, you need, most of all, to give yourself permission to do what you already know about. You need to unrepress yourself and do what comes naturally, and without worrying so much about the possible consequences. Tell the sex police, inside and outside your head, to shut up and accept what you have done, both before and after you do it, as a perfectly normal expression of good feeling between two people.

Looking for Specific Emotional Causes

Specific causes for sexual difficulties include guilty thoughts and thoughts about sin, neophilia (always wanting something new), hostility toward him, and jealousy.

Identifying and Reducing Guilt

Guilt can take a direct form, the familiar harsh conscience, or appear as sexual guilt equivalents, which are nonverbal expressions of a harsh punitive conscience. Such expressions can include not only the major sexual problems discussed above, but also more minor sexual problems, which, dynamically speaking, are compromises that allow you a measure of fun and success as long as the sexual fun isn't too much and the success is limited and incomplete. These sexual compromises are a way to make the statement that, "It's OK to do it as long as I don't like it too much or do it too well." They satisfy the pangs of conscience, but they also send the partner off-putting messages, such as, "I don't like your leading me into temptation." Examples include modest performance difficulties such as:

- Losing and gaining an erection occasionally during sex.
- Impatience—a desire to get it over with as soon as possible.
- Aftermath regrets and disgust where you cannot wait to wash off or have to run to the refrigerator to drink orange juice to clear the palate.

In chapter 9, I discussed how self-homophobia negatively affects your relationships. Self-homophobia also affects your sex life. It often accompanies guilt and thoughts about sin. Self-homophobia can originate when others' hatred of you becomes self-hatred, or in a native, in-built antagonism to your sexual desires. Self-homophobia typically causes gay men to split love and sex, putting a "lover" on a pedestal and only being able to have great sex with a devalued partner, someone they don't even like personally—like a pick-up they never fully intend to see again. The thinking goes as follows: "Sex is bad; however it's OK if I mess it up in some significant way, and one good way to do that is to have it with someone I neither like nor admire."

Some gay men become especially self-homophobic when they meet a new lover. This becomes the occasion to start thinking about the "unnaturalness" of gay sex because it becomes the occasion to think of the downside of being gay itself, like not having any children and so not being able to pass on your genes to future generations. It's as if the more intense the feeling, the more intense the guilt.

Everything fired up his conscience and turned it against Pat, a gay man devoted to the church, who was unable to have sex with his lover because, as he put it, he loved him too much to sully him that way. He described his problem in almost semireligious terms. Having sex with a lover, but not with an anonymous partner, made him feel as though he went from the cloth to the blacklist, and "as if I were the first man since Moses to break all Ten Commandments at once."

Closely associated with guilt are thoughts about sin. A common one is an intrusive thought, typically occurring right on schedule, that it is a sin to have an orgasm.

In my patient Barry's case, the thought "It's a sin to have an orgasm," was a continuation of the thought he had as an adolescent when he first masturbated: "Don't do that again." Later in life, this thought flowed through his brain, short-circuiting it during sex, making it difficult, and sometimes impossible, for him to have an orgasm. This was because the thought spread to become a hesitation to touch and use certain body parts—particularly the anus, something that he would "never do."

Therapeutically, anything that diminishes guilt and feelings of sin can enhance sexual performance. The process of diminishing guilt and sin basically involves:

- Learning to live with and love yourself without expecting yourself to be perfect.
- Accepting that you are gay, 100 percent.
- Accepting that you have a body, and bodily needs.

Dealing with a Constant Need for Newness

Guilt and the feeling you have sinned isn't all of it though. Compromised performance with someone you already know, even someone you just met, can also be due to neophilia, the need to have somebody new at all times. In popular terms, this is often called, "the seven year itch." Neophiliacs tend to complain a lot about the stultifying effects of overfamiliarity. They get restless and dislike all the predictability and repetition of sex with the same man. They like cruising challenges, for success here proves their desirability over and over again. For this and other reasons, instead of old love, which for them soon becomes uninteresting, they prefer new love, which for them doesn't last.

In good relationships, when a changeover from new to old occurs, Mr. New Collectible becomes Mr. Valuable Antique. In neophiliacs this doesn't happen, and it doesn't happen not because of something inherent in gay sex, but due to some personal and interpersonal conflict. We hear, "The relationship died because of my problem with sex," when in fact the sex died because of a problem with the relationship.

Overcoming neophilia means recognizing that wonderful sexually intense ecstatic abdominal orgasms with the feeling that you are melting into your handsome new lover do tend to diminish with time, but so what. Old sex is different from, not worse than, new sex. Indeed, the thrills of old sex, though different, are just as great, if not greater, than the thrills of new sex. The solution is to learn to accept the differences as evolutionary changes for the better and not to find a new man, but to improve your relationship with the old one.

Dealing with Hostility

Hostility is another cause of performance difficulties. Boredom, impotence, and promiscuity are partly put into place, usually without your knowing it, to hurt the man you love, as when you send him the message, "One man, and that means you, is not enough." Perhaps you actually enjoy making your partner work hard, or even defeating his best efforts.

To overcome hostility, become more accepting of him (short of tolerating abuse for the sake of a relationship). Think about his wonders, avoid thinking about his shortcomings, and recognize that as the relationship progresses, if you love him and he loves you, he will change for you and each of you will become just what the other wants him to be.

Dealing with Jealousy

Jealousy is another common reason for performance difficulties. Jealousy makes you impotent if, having already decided that he is cheating on you, you are in no mood to satisfy him, or if you are in a mood, it is the mood to cheat back. Developing basic trust takes the edge off unfounded suspicions, and that reduces your desire to cheat. It also stops a vicious cycle where he cheats because he thinks you don't like him as evidenced by your not trusting him, which gives you less reason to trust him, more reason to cheat, and so on.

Asking Him to Change, When Indicated

Perhaps your sexual problems are not mainly or entirely yours. It is possible that your performance difficulties are just an understandable, and not surprising, response to what he is, or is not, doing with and to you.

What about his technique? Is there inadequate friction or is there adequate pressure? Does he avoid a part of your body that you would like to have stimulated? Does he let his teeth get in the way? Is he unable to suppress the gag reflex for emotional reasons or because of lack of motivation? Not enough appreciation is often the big enemy of orgasm. Does he tell you, directly or indirectly, what a great gorgeous potent man you are, or is he indifferent to you in so many ways? Does he actually criticize your endowments and abilities?

Clearly, the remedy for Max's impotence was not only up to Max. It was also up to Charles, Max's lover. Max was in treatment in part because he was impotent. One reason was that he hated it when his lover Charles watched pornography. He felt rejected, but he was too embarrassed, and too shy and fearful too, to complain. So he said instead, "It doesn't matter," over and over again before finally coming out with how he really felt.

Charles also rankled Max by reporting his dreams to Max the morning after he had them. Max knew what they meant, and that they were hardly flattering. Here is an example: "I was riding on a train trying to get to you, but the train kept going in the wrong direction, past beautiful scenery, past beautiful mountains, much prettier than where I was ticketed to go—it was just taking me along and I couldn't get off because it wouldn't stop." Max didn't have to be Freud to be insulted. Charles also criticized Max whenever he did something wrong. Instead of supporting him, he called him stupid. That lowered Max's spirits, and something else, too.

Max's impotence wasn't mainly due to "poor technique" or "diffidence." It was mainly his response to the way Charles treated him. It was also his way to get back at Charles to make him feel as crestfallen as Max felt: a once strutting bird now with its head down, scratching the earth in abject humiliation.

Of course, people like Max can be hypersensitive. They can feel that congratulations are in order for anything positive that they do, especially anything beyond the call of duty. But people like Charles are pushing people like Max too far. I always thought that Charles was why Max started wearing a T-shirt that says, "You are the reason I am medicated."

Selfishness is right up there, too, as a reason for a partner's impotence. People like to get as much as they give. It's exciting, it's stimulating, and if they sense that a relationship is one way, they get turned off.

John, William's lover, would ask William, a personal friend of mine, "What do you want to do?" but then he would not do it, because he really didn't listen to, or care about, William's answer. As a self-oriented person, he also wanted it all and wanted it now. He wanted anal sex constantly and often woke William up in the middle of the night trying to have it, even when William, reminding him that his big break on Broadway tomorrow meant that he needed all the sleep he could get, asked him not to. John was also overly critical when William didn't meet his performance specifications exactly. He refused to yield and make tradeoffs, refusing William anal sex in his turn, then claiming that he couldn't do it because it was morally wrong. William was willing to subordinate his needs to John's desires, but only up to a point. Beyond that he would punish John by not performing adequately. As William put it, "I am getting back at him for always needing to come first, both figuratively and literally."

Sexual difficulties arising in interpersonal problems like those I just described are best resolved by setting limits on, and asking for what you want from, a partner directly, not passive-aggressively by complaining and undermining. Ask your partner to be more giving and more supportive. During the discussion, make it clear that you are not picking on him, but are only trying to make a better bed for the both of you to lie in.

An Action Plan
Here are some things to do to improve your sexual performance.

Save It Up for a While
That is not unthinkable even for gay men, and it can be enough. Yes, masturbation is a release, but you want to be captured. Don't go for quantity; go for quality. Many times, performance is improved just by waiting a few days in between attempts. The excitement is greater, in part because the pressure builds and that stimulates the nerves.

Consider Newer Medications for Erectile Problems
I don't really recommend pharmacological aphrodisiacs. In my experience, they don't work very well, and if they work at all it is only by irritating sensitive

membranes. You can accomplish the same thing by natural methods such as decreasing performance frequency and by choosing a partner who is accepting of you. Acceptance is discussed more below. In special cases, you may want to consult your doctor about the use of Viagra.

Work on Being More Seductive

A lot of little things can mean a lot. The kind of shoes or underwear both of you wear, the use, or nonuse, of deodorant or toilet water, the beard and haircut, the glasses, the posture, the weight and the muscles (or lack of them) can make a great deal of difference when it comes to sexual attraction, and fortunately these things can all be improved on. Find out what he wants, not what you think he might like, and act accordingly.

Improve the Mechanics of the Sex Act Directly

There may be emotional reasons for not bearing down hard enough, and they may be a paradigm for your life itself, but, before resorting to complex psychological remedies, try some simpler ones. Try to work a little harder, move a little faster, breathe a little less, and, most of all, put the pressure on. He will succeed if only you try harder. Of course there are sexual aids, and you can find out all about these by going into one of the sexually oriented "chain" stores, but I don't advocate using those any more than I advocate wearing a girdle when you should instead be losing weight.

Find a Reassuring, Accepting Lover

The best lover for impotent men is one who couldn't care less if you can't do it tonight. Reassurance enhances performance. Retarded orgasm or an inability to get and keep an erection get worse when he nags, cajoles, complains, and threatens you unless you get and keep it up—for that only puts you, and it, down. Performance difficulties often disappear as if by magic when a partner develops positive personality characteristics like the ones I describe throughout this book, when he becomes more flexible, selfless, empathic, undemanding, and forbearing. That makes him both figuratively and literally easier to love. Enduring sexual fantasies that have merely wilted because you haven't recently aired, or watered, them are best revived not mechanically but emotionally, by a partner's acceptance of you. That elicits the fantasy of melting into him and becoming one with his secretions and his body, and that helps you have an orgasm that symbolizes your weeping for joy and gratitude.

Be Patient

Just as the best partners don't get impatient with you, you shouldn't get impatient with yourself. It didn't work? Get over it. This wasn't your debut at Carnegie Hall. The critics weren't at the performance, and you get another chance, even sooner than you think, like an hour from now.

Don't Let Nonsexual Problems into Bed with You

Don't feel so guilty about being gay or about your specific sexual desires. You won't need the Ready or any other kind of Whip if you aren't so ashamed of yourself, and if you don't feel you need to be punished for who you are and what you want. Don't buy into others' criticisms of what you do.

Accept all your successes, sexual and otherwise, without feeling that you should fail because success is undeserved or forbidden. It helps to remember the T-shirt that says, "God made me gay," then do what is God's will and gift to you. It helps to tell yourself that if sex is a natural function, and if homosexuality is simply a variant of normal, like being redheaded or left-handed, then, biblical-style injunctions aside, abstinence is not an option, and, certainly within a committed relationship, sex, like anything else good, should be done both right and often.

Break through specific inhibitions and willingly do anything he wants you to do as long as it doesn't affect your mental or physical health. What affects your mental health? Humiliations and hurtful behaviors directed to you that make you cringe. What affects your physical health? Unprotected sex with a partner who is HIV positive, anything that hurts or injures you, like fisting, or inserting your tongue into his anus. If it doesn't feel good, or it feels good but you know it isn't smart, don't go along. Then become able to enjoy yourself, without regret, and give yourself permission to be imperfect from time to time.

Avoid Certain Remedies That Can Hurt More Than They Help

In my clinical experience, the use of pornography often creates the very difficulties it was designed to cure. Many self-help books recommend, in addition to the feather and the whipped cream and sex in the garden under the gardenias, watching pornographic movies while doing it (all that makes you too busy to actually do it, doesn't it?). Bringing out the sex toys and playing "Spanish Inquisition" doesn't do a thing for me. I am completely turned off, and even offended, by someone who thinks I am so undesirable that they have to get turned on by a food, a feather, a fetish, and a flick, just so that they can use me to climax. Advice columnists to the contrary, it's not OK to get into the habit of fantasizing about other men when you do it with him. Thinking of the bus boy when you are doing it with your lover is not focusing on the task at hand. It is doing something halfway without giving it your full attention. Lovers know when your mind is elsewhere, especially when your free-flowing fantasy leads you to slip during sex and call the boy for service.

In conclusion, tight blue jeans, sultry surroundings, sexy disco tapes, and the like make sex exotic. Permanency and love, which are the best aphrodisiacs of them all, make sex erotic.

Once you have overcome any sexual difficulties you might have, you can perform well both sexually and in those important areas of your interpersonal relationships that are closely linked to sexual performance. You are now as free of sexual inhibitions as you are of personal inhibitions, and the other way around. You are now as sexy out of bed as in it. Of course, sexual problems can come back and you may have to put the principles in this section to work more than once.

Seeking Professional Help

Formal psychotherapy takes time and money, and is a big commitment, so before assuming that you have a deep emotional problem, try improving your skill sets. That may be enough to be successful in your quest for love.

Also consider the possibility of just trying to wait out a difficult period. I know of many gay men who think one day they are dying from all the grief and the next day spot Mr. New and just ring out Mr. Old. Although there are some exceptions, as a rule, if you are making any progress at all, patience might be indicated. If possible, give yourself six to twelve months before entering treatment.

You should seek help immediately if you are suffering from a prolonged or serious depression that is:

- Robbing you of much enjoyment in life.
- Keeping you from forming new relationships.
- Causing you to act in self-destructive ways.
- Making you feel suicidal.

Mark, a patient of mine, was depressed his whole life. The second part of his double depression started when his lover left him. Now he found himself staring into space, refusing to go out of the house. He even refused to part the curtains, feeling, "Why bother, there isn't anything out on the street worth looking at anyway." Mark blamed himself entirely for what went wrong and punished himself harshly for not having done enough to prevent it. Mark improved a great deal just with a little attention. He said that the initial improvement gave him hope that his depression would be over soon.

Here are some other possible indications for seeking outside therapy:

- You are stalled, or things are getting worse for you. Last year you met a few people; now you aren't meeting anyone at all.
- You are extremely lonely and could use a substitute relationship to relieve your isolation.
- Your response to the loss of a prior lover is an overreaction, perversely independent of the quality of the relationship or the length of time it lasted.

- You find yourself acting impulsively.
- You are making bad choices on the rebound, getting involved again before you are ready, picking anybody just to have somebody.
- You are stalking an old lover, calling and cajoling him into getting together with you again, following him everywhere and even spying on him, unable to deny his negative feelings toward you and the problem that led to the breakup in the first place.
- You find yourself accepting bad advice from family and friends who keep telling you to do things that aren't in your best interests.
- You are confused about a lot of things or need help in clarifying and sorting out a specific, very complex situation.

Morris and Ken, two patients of mine, both needed to be in therapy because they were having problems with each other and with their son. They adopted a son at the beginning of an eighteen-year relationship, then the two of them broke up and are now sharing custody. One man is Dad, the other is Papa, and the boy divides his time between the two. The kid accepts having two dads, and even the divorce, but he makes Morris and Ken miserable because he cannot handle their new lovers. He thinks they threaten to come between the kid and Daddy and Papa. Morris's and Ken's new relationships were strained as a result and their new lovers were threatening to leave unless things calmed down and sorted themselves out.

I recommended a few "former-family" sessions. During them, we worked out problems with anger and feelings of disappointment and abandonment, enabling all concerned to look forward to a future full of new, loving relationships.

Getting into Therapy

If you have tried everything and feel you would benefit from a course of therapy, by all means find a therapist who will help you reach your goal of finding a meaningful and lasting relationship. Seeking help from others, even from a therapist, isn't an act of defeat. Rather, effective psychotherapy can be just one more ray in a beam of light to guide you on your way.

When selecting a therapist you will want to look for someone who will:
- Be there for you when you need him
- Be an inspiration to you
- Act as a good role model for you
- Encourage you to find someone for yourself
- Focus on and deal with the actual problem you are having, not some theoretical difficulty you don't have

Charles, a patient of mine, spent a small fortune on sessions with a psychic astrologer, who also used a specialized breathing technique designed to help him cope with loneliness. He liked this woman—and why not? She avoided exploring his contribution to his isolation, like his extreme involvement in chat rooms on the Internet and his close relationship with his dog. She never helped him face the fact that he was alone partly because of his anxieties and partly because he was beginning to lose his social abilities. I saw him in short-term therapy, and told him that, like everybody else, he already knew how to breathe. I thought that what he needed to know was where the off switch was on his computer, and the location of a good kennel to board his dog while he went somewhere away from it all for a pleasant and productive week of looking around. He made a clean break by going away on a little trip, and he actually met someone there who was just right for him.

The best therapists are affirmative, that is, supportive and noncritical, yet strike a balance between reducing your guilt by absolving you of all responsibility for your problems and your fate, and taking you to task for everything that might have happened in your life.

In order to get the most out of help in any form, self-help or psychotherapy, you'll want to be honest with—and about—yourself. Look in the mirror, register what you see there, and report what you have discovered. Don't blame yourself for everything, but do try to understand yourself, at least enough to learn what and how things went wrong in your life. Study your interaction with the world, then make changes by taking action.

Avoid making all the mistakes on your own. Ask questions and listen to the answers about what the right course of action might be. Accept that no therapist (or self-help book) is perfect. Nobody has all the answers. Because trial and error is part of many experiences, things can go wrong before they go right, and even the other way around. So when things aren't going that well, keep at it until things work out for you.

It won't help you to get angry, resentful, defensive, or blame the very people who are trying to be honest with you. Be like the good employee who learns from, rather than is insulted by, his job evaluations.

Don't be like Sheldon, a very defensive patient of mine, whom no one, me especially, could tell he looked ridiculous wearing a shirt whose vertical stripes outlined each fold of an overly pendulous belly. I kept telling Sheldon, who couldn't meet anyone even though he was beautiful, rich, and talented, my opinions on why he was still single. He disagreed with everything I said and gave me an argument, too. Now you know part of the reason why he is still single.

One last caveat: unless absolutely necessary, don't take medication before you are certain you need it. Lonely gay men can be depressed and depressed gay men sometimes find therapists who recommend medication for a chemical imbalance. Make sure your chemical imbalance, if you have one, is primary, not secondary to any stress you might be under. As you already know from your adolescent acne, there is nothing like emotional turmoil to throw your body off balance chemically, and nothing like success in relationships to create less stress, correcting that chemical imbalance.

The next chapter involves putting it all together and getting started. In this chapter, I offer you a practical, action-oriented approach. I help you take what you have learned so far and develop a life plan from the points of my book that are right for you. I help you decide which suggestions *you* find helpful and productive and put them to work. Success may not come tomorrow or even this year. There is an element of luck, and individual variations are important, too. But I just bet that if you go about looking for love actively and in all the right ways, you will find, almost without being aware of it, that sooner or later love will come looking for you.

11

Put It All Together and Get Started

You have read about the nine steps toward finding a loving relationship. Now it's time to choreograph these steps into a dance. You've spent the last months thinking about your love life. Now's the time to start falling in love. You've taken one step at a time. Now's the time to start leaping up that staircase. You have learned how to fish. Now's the time to get out on the water and try your hand at the bait, the lure, the reel, and the rod. You have read about all the right strokes. Now is the time to get past putting your toe in the water and start swimming.

Act before You Think

Together we have been thinking a lot about you, your actions, and the results you have, or haven't, been getting. Now it's time to stop thinking and start doing. By now, you should have the emotional tools you need to take the process from the top and start the action going. There may still be some myths you buy into, and some personal inhibitions you have to being successful. But you can work around those. Think of them as a pile on your desk that you can safely ignore for now, so that you can do the most important work of your life without getting bogged down in minutiae.

Here's the principle behind my advice. I once had a patient who wasn't paying his bills. When I asked him for money he told me, "Doc, I would pay you except for the fact that I have an inhibition about paying you and that's why I am here in the first place." I told him that that symptom might be the last to go, and in the meantime I needed to be paid. I asked him to pay me first so that we could work on his tightfistedness next. It's the same with you. Your guilt about success, your loneliness, and your shyness about speaking to strangers might be the last symptom to go. Meanwhile, you cannot just rot there waiting for an epiphany. Now's the moment to start putting your plan into practice, even though you aren't entirely ready for prime time. Just putting these steps into practice will help you open up new avenues of thought, identify and conquer new anxieties, raise certain problems that need solving, and ask certain questions that need answering.

Get Some Real Successes under Your Belt

Real successes under your belt make you feel good about yourself. They give you the courage, spirit, and desire to go on and be even more successful. Remember that you are strengthening skills here. Just as you build muscles at that gym I'm always encouraging you to join and use, you build muscles of communication by dealing with rejection, and being in a relationship. How do you get to the Carnegie Hall of Love? Practice, practice, practice.

Make Relationships Paramount

Look on everything with a jaundiced eye. I used to know a doctor who worked in the emergency room. Whenever he got a new admission he didn't see "patient," he saw "malpractice suit." I am recommending the same idea, but with a different context, to you. See "possible husband" in every morsel of food and drink you order, every airline ticket you buy, and every hotel reservation you make. Forget about pleasure for it's own sake. Each and every activity should be put into a relationship context. You don't just go to the theatre to see the play; you go to the theatre to be part of the scene—and that includes what goes on with the other theatre goers.

If you have an apartment, go through it item by item and evaluate everything in it to see if it helps you meet a man. I am sure you have thought of things from other perspectives, like does that beautiful bearskin rug just out of House

Gorgeous flatter my living room? But have you thought of things from the perspective of what they might do for your relationships? Maybe that rug goes with that shrunken head on the wall, but maybe they both turn your new man, that cute vegetarian, off.

This is part of the important process of self-motivation focused not on the perspective of your aesthetics, or of your finances, but of your relationships. It's a new way of thinking that you can develop—a relationship-oriented approach to life—and the sooner you do that the faster you will do things not for yourself but for him. It takes practice. The first hundred times you will forget to ask yourself what this act or behavior means for a relationship, but soon you will get the hang of it, and it will become your second nature.

It also helps for you to be clear to others about where you stand. Things you do with others should be evaluated the same way. Are we going out tonight together just to have a good dinner or are we going out tonight to meet a good man? Know in advance: what happens if I meet someone and you don't? Will you beat up on me, making me more depressed than I need to be at this time of my life? Will you stick your nose in and mess it up, or will you just vanish into the shadows and call me up the next day eager to know if it's finally Him? Think these things through before you go out so that you don't make a mess of the evening afterwards. Set the ground rules from the beginning. This is where my head is, and this is what you can expect from me. If this happens, then I will do that. After all, you are now not just "big sister," or platonic lover, but relationship maven.

Develop a Newly Positive Mind-set

Develop the new mind-set that nothing can stop you now. Act as if that is the case, even if it's only half true. Put these steps into action and they will work for you even if you only half-believe in them.

The basic principle is that you can usually do what you think you can do, and you usually cannot do what you think is impossible. The most important principle of your new mind-set is to keep at it. The harder you try, the more you work at finding Mr. Right, the quicker you are likely to meet him. Finding the partner of a lifetime requires devotion as well as skill. This book can help you develop your skill sets, but it is up to you to become excited about using them. Remember, you are embarking on a wonderful adventure.

Become Very Patient

Don't worry if, at first, these steps do not seem to work for you all at once. You may have to try them again and again until you see even a little change. Some people are very lucky from the start. Others just have to keep at it until something goes right. I have had some patients give up prematurely on one or more of these nine steps. They say they tried but it didn't work. So what? Try it again. Next time it may come out right. In fact, each of these nine steps may have to be repeated hundreds of times before Mr. Right comes on the horizon. It's only a problem if you think it is and give up because you get discouraged. We all have to do new things more than once before they become second nature. Try taking one step at a time, and try leaping up the whole staircase to the top. Also try falling down (without hurting yourself) and having to pick yourself up again to start over. You have the inclination, you have the time, and you have the opportunity, so use what you have to work out the approach that is best for you.

Release the Energy You Have in You

Be energetic about finding Mr. Right, because the basic energy principle is that energy releases energy. It's the tautology of life: you get started and you keep going simply because you have gotten started and kept going. Changing your life around is like getting up in the morning. You can get out of bed if you get out of bed and force yourself to stay up. The same thing is true for finding love. You will find it faster and better if you get excited. Excitement is a great source of energy that feeds on itself and keeps you going. Exciting things happen when you get excited. Powerful changes occur when you turn on the power. An old term that still has some descriptive value describes what you are doing: "psyching yourself up."

Structure Your Life

Do all the things you need to do and have put off doing until now. Go to the doctor for a checkup and the dentist to fix your teeth. Have you been tested for AIDS? Have you discussed safe sex with your physician? Go to charm school and take a course on how to meet men—especially if you can find a class that favors hands-on intramural practice. Create. Start writing or painting—it occupies time and, if you get serious and professional about it, brings you into contact with others similarly inclined. That doesn't mean doing busy work that might divert you from your goals. It means having one eye on the canvass and the other on your upcoming art exhibition where they will throw themselves all over you and think you are cute because you are famous.

Tailor a Plan to You

Now that you're committed to applying these steps with energy and enthusiasm, you'll want to create a plan with an approach that is right for you, one that is applicable to your preferences and capacities, to your special, perhaps unique, situation. What do you do first? Do you have to do everything to make it all come out right, or can you cut a few corners? We are all different, so won't different guys have different procedures to follow? Aren't some of us single for one reason, some of us for another? Does the same plan apply to someone who is just starting out in gay life as it does to someone who has just left a relationship or had one go sour on him?

I encourage you to approach the planning process in little pieces. If it helps you, go back through the nine steps and underline what is most important to you. Yes, you will be soiling the pages, but don't treat the book like a beautiful man who is gorgeous but useless. The book is a practical manual, not a museum piece, so mark it up as much as you need to. Then use your markings to extract a written plan that is right for you—specifically for *your* personality and *your* situation. Clearly, gay men who are shy and cannot bring themselves to say hello to a stranger have different problems and needs and require different solutions than gay men who are bold to a fault. Hunks need a different world view than those of us who are not drop-dead gorgeous. Your unique personality and situation will determine which parts of the book are significant and meaningful for you and which parts you can soft-pedal or safely ignore. Here's one attempt to organize the material according to different theoretical situations.

Just Divorced and the Divorce Has Been Messy

You are depressed and lonely but you probably don't have many obstacles to cruising—after all you have been there, done that, and have even done it surprisingly well. For you, the most relevant parts of the book are those relating to being born all over again—how to overcome loneliness, lethargy, inertia, and low self-esteem, and be a successful self-starter.

Just Divorced and the Divorce Was a Welcome End to Ten Years of Unspeakable Bliss

You are probably unmotivated due to pessimism about relationships. Instead of remaining vulnerable to buying into all the myths about gay relationships, read and reread my section on facts versus fancies of gay life.

You Are Just Out

You are very young, or you are first coming out at an advancing age. Your chief enemy may be ignorance of how to go about doing things. Reread the section on where to go to find him, and all the other sections that are geared to giving you the facts and the skills you need to help you overcome emotional impediments to using the capacities you already have.

You also may be impulsive and promiscuous. If so, you do not need to overcome inhibitions as much as you need a few more. So read the sections that involve becoming more realistic and calm, especially the sections on the dark sides of promiscuity.

You may also be impressionable, thinking that everyone you come across who is Mr. Available is Mr. Right. Focus on the sections that tell you who is better and who is best in a man.

Also, you are probably floundering about who you are, and the best way to present yourself. Focus on those sections in my book that tell you about being Mr. Right for him so that he can be Mr. Right for you.

You Have Been Lonely for What Seems Like Forever

Maybe you are about to give up and get another ten cats. This problem may require the most extensive work of all. You have to overcome inhibitions, you may have to change how you look, and you will probably have to do a lot of pushing to overcome inertia, distractions, and low self-esteem. Step Nine, overcoming obstacles, is the one for you to focus on for now, as is the section on myths that say you should be pessimistic about looking for Mr. Right.

You Are Getting Older

If you are older, there is a whole section for you. But don't skip the other sections or the steps in them. You are just an older version of all the younger men described in this book, so refer to the sections applicable to the specific situation you are in—just over a divorce, just coming out, and so on.

You Are Long or Short on Attributes

Your goals should be tailored, at least to an extent, to reflect your good attributes. These can determine the specific parameters of your goals. After all, you shouldn't apply for a job as rocket scientist if you have an advanced degree in theater or ballet.

Create a Paper Trail

Don't think that making documents about your life—lists, self-evaluations, decision trees, and the like—is too much work or a big waste of time.

Written documents keep you from doing things impressionistically. They focus you on what you are doing and keep you from doing it in an altered state—flying without having actually gotten off the ground. There is nothing so real as words on paper, and there is nothing so unreal as a gay man out of control acting first and regretting it next.

One night a week (at the least) come home and work on your documents. Update them. It will force you to think a little about what just happened in your life. You will be more or less constrained to evaluate your actions and your progress on a regular basis. Things on the page help you *reflect*. You would be surprised how many gay men never reflect on their actions. They read about what to do, and they do it, but they don't stop and think about what they are doing, or have done. That flattens the learning curve.

When evaluating your overall progress answer the following questions and change course accordingly:

1) Am I any closer to meeting Mr. Right now than I was a month ago?

   Yes: I met three men, one of whom interests me a lot.

   If this is the case, no action on your part is presently necessary. Go to Question 2.

   No: I'm still going home alone every night, except for Silas who is no big deal.
   If this is the case, do some or all of the action-oriented things in this chapter and in the rest of this book. Now go to Question 4.

2) Why am I closer to my goals?

   I am closer because a month ago I didn't say hello to anybody but waited for them to say hello to me. Now I smile and wink and say hello to everybody. Out of a hundred men, half say hello back and half of those stop and start a conversation with me. So that's why I only had two possibles and now I have three maybes and one looks good. Also, I stopped feeling sorry for myself. I gave up getting drunk every night, and I took out that ring from my tongue so that I could better appeal to Mr. Traditional.

3) What can I do to get even closer?

I can push a little harder and a little more often, and instead of selecting men I really don't like because I think that is all I can get, the next time I can and will approach Mr. Right.

4) What didn't I do that still has to be done?

I didn't speak to the one I really wanted because I was afraid he would reject me. Next time I will do better and if I see him again I will go over to him and ask him if I can buy him a drink.

5) What did I do that I shouldn't have done?

I did walk over to that humpy number like the hussy that I used to be and told him how cute he was, and what I would like to do about it.

6) Where do I want to be next month and the month after that?

Next month I want to be a little closer to Tim and see if John works out too.

7) What is my ideal here?

A wedding ring from Tim.

8) What is my reasonable goal and expectation here?

An invitation to dinner from Tim and a hint or two about another possible engagement, the kind that comes with invitations.

Making a schedule book and a diary helps you evaluate your progress and see some progress when you are moving slowly. To avoid getting discouraged and deciding it's quitting time, review all the little triumphs in your notes. It will help you magnify and zoom in on what progress you are making. Especially if your progress is slow, do a year-to-year in addition to a month-to-month self-evaluation. You would be surprised how things that look the same from one month to another change over a year without your even noticing it. It can be a terrific morale booster when you feel yourself stalled and in the doldrums to discover that things are progressing faster than you thought.

Schedule Yourself

If your schedule is empty, stare for a moment at all the blank pages. Your goal is to scribble on as many as possible. Start to fill them up. You will be proud of how well you are doing, and you will be in a better mood than before, prompting you to fill them up even more. Use a thick black felt pen. You can best chart your progress if you compare the amount of dark ink on today's pages with the amount of dark ink on yesterday's pages. The thick black pen makes you look busier than you might actually be.

Your goal is to have a schedule book that will please you and be the envy of all your "sisters." Never mind that for now you don't have *him*. You are getting a full schedule, and that means you are on your way to having a full life.

What should be on your schedule? Anything for now, as long as you are out of the house. You shouldn't be at home by yourself much. If you don't have a lover, you should be out there looking for one. If you live with your parents, you should be getting over that and moving out as soon as possible. Every empty page on your schedule book says one thing only: you aren't doing what you could be doing, so your life is in danger of becoming as empty as the page.

Try some things you presently hate. Hate is an irrational emotion. It's like the four-year-old who refuses to eat a new food because he says he hates it when he's never even tasted it before. So force yourself to do exactly what you dread doing or have dismissed from your mind. You will probably discover a whole new world of wonderful activities, and men, out there just for you.

Make a list consisting of five things you haven't done before. Do you hate opera? Night at the City Center is for you. Don't go there and you will miss a whole group of guys who do. Do you hate bars? Gussy yourself up and go out to one to see what it is that you might be missing. Walk in and want to walk out again? Stay put, tough it out, and enjoy the scene, remembering that it changes from hour to hour.

Learn as You Yearn

Try to learn from your disasters. Don't wake up the next morning thinking that last night was such a mess that life is over. Say to yourself, "I have just taken a course in survival, and to pass the finals I have to learn from the experience." We all have situations where we haven't succeeded. So, first do something, then see how well it worked. If it did work ask why (just because something works doesn't mean you cannot learn something from it). If it didn't work, ask why too, and apply what you learned to the next time. That either means you have to try the same thing again but differently, or that you have to change your approach.

This is a practical manual that recognizes that putting anything new into practice means doing it more than once. Most things you cannot get right the first time. You couldn't play the "Minute Waltz" the first time you saw it, and you cannot play the dating and mating games the first time you try. Don't give up. The last time I looked, I saw enough men to assure you that you have the opportunity of trying out new things, and making all the mistakes, until you get it and your life right.

Deal Effectively with Crossroads

Whenever you are uncertain of what path to take, pull out that notepad and make a flow chart—you know, the kind you make when you are tracing your ancestors back to the Vikings.

You have no men in your life and you are trying to figure out how to get a man. Or you have one man in your life and you are trying to determine if he is right for you to continue to pursue, or marry. Or you have two men in your life and you are trying to decide between them. To make that hard-nosed reality decision, you have to create a list with two columns, one with the positives and the other with the negatives. If I had made such a list some years ago, I would have spared myself some very self-destructive acrobatics:

Should I move to San Francisco to be with Frank?

Positive: A lawyer. Gorgeous blonde, with a little help from the elements. Great in bed, and all systems go.

Negative: I have to move to Boston and he doesn't want to move there with me, but instead prefers to go to San Francisco. Now that he lives in San Francisco, he tells me he met a six-foot tall, blond Scandinavian from

Colorado there and is otherwise preoccupied. Drinks too much. Was quite obese but now has lost a lot of weight, but he may put it back from eating too much of what he considers to be the perfect vegetable: carrot cake.

If I had made a list like this I would have stayed in Boston and not moved to San Francisco to be with Frank.

Can you imagine giving up my professional career and personal life for Frank if I had actually made such a list and read the items on it? Perhaps, if I were beyond crazy in love and just crazy. But I didn't make such a list so I never got real or sensible. Without the list I took from Column A and forgot all about Column B.

Get All Caught Up in the Excitement of Change

A good place to start is by being a big helpful "sister" to someone else, someone who needs you. There is nothing that helps you attain your goals like helping others attain theirs. I know from being a therapist that I often do the good things I come up with to tell my patients to do. Sometimes I am surprised what comes out of my mouth, how useful it is, and how it applies to me as well as to them. You will be surprised too. As you talk to other men and give them good advice, some of it rubs off on you, and you take your own advice. After all it's free, and it comes from someone reliable (I hope). Besides, why should they have something good that you don't have too. You would be surprised how you can sort things out for yourself just by sorting them out for others.

Get Some Help from Others

Find a therapist-substitute. Find a "sister" with a big heart and an even bigger ear and discuss your progress with him. Get his feedback. Have him read this book too so that he knows where you are coming from. Follow his advice after being certain that it is good advice for you.

As I was in the process of researching this book, I interviewed a number of men at the semi-gay restaurant that I frequent. At first I thought that they wouldn't be interested in talking to me. Then I realized that it's wise to never underestimate the sociability of some gay men. They were interested and actually eager to tell me what they thought. In fact, I almost couldn't eat my dinner from all the discussion going on. Next I thought: so many gay men who cannot meet Mr. Right go through life in isolation, thinking they are the only ones who have this problem and ashamed of having it. As a result they don't even think to talk to others about it and ask their advice. In the earlier parts of this book, I suggested you ask others their opinion about how you look and act. Here I suggest you zoom in on obviously coupled men and ask them how they got to be that way. Where did they meet? How did it happen? How did they connect? What mistakes did they make before they connected? What would they do again if they had the chance and what wouldn't they repeat? This is a technique that you can develop and use for a lifetime. It's one that you can continue to employ after you have finished reading this book and are out there on your own. It will also keep the ideas in this book fresh in your mind as you see what others have tried and what helped them. Don't be ashamed of wanting or needing to know. Ask away. People love to talk about themselves and you will learn a lot if you just listen. I bet they have some practical advice that helps you improve your chances of success.

Moving Forward

In conclusion, I urge you to take on the special techniques in this book that together make up my action-oriented plan, one that consists of:
- Ignoring discouraging myths
- Correcting silly illogical thoughts about your self-worth and your chances
- Choosing the right man while staying flexible about who exactly that might be
- Fine-tuning your strategies and tactics
- Maximizing your looks, good personal qualities, and sexual abilities
- Knowing where to go to meet him and how to worm your way into his heart once you get there
- Overcoming internal psychological obstacles to success, obstacles such as

inertia, the paralyzing pain of loneliness, fear of rejection, love-aversive tendencies, low self-esteem, self-homophobia, and a tendency to get distracted when you should be working on your relationships

Apply these techniques in real time and continue applying them in an ongoing way to create a *modus vivendi* for the rest of your life. I gave you that fish when you were starving. Now I am teaching you how to fish to keep you forever in sushi.

Believe me, it's not impossible to meet Mr. Wonderful. I did it, after years and years of trying and making all the mistakes, and I did it at a pretty advanced age too. If I can do it, so can you. I did it partly through luck but mainly through effort, and that involved making some really big personal changes. The steps outlined in this book will help you head in the right direction and get where you want to go. As you proceed, you will be discovering the greatest truth of them all: that a committed relationship is paradise, and that this is a paradise that is both available to you and within your grasp, right here on earth.

Appendix

A Short Guide to a Lasting Gay Relationship

As you go out in search of Mr. Right, it will be helpful for you to refresh for yourself the paths you need to take and the warning signs you need to be on the watch for. The following is a short summary of the lessons you have learned in this book. I suggest that you consult this section regularly, and if you come across an idea that that seems hazy, or that you have forgotten completely, go back and reread that section of the book.

Finding Mr. Right

Finding and connecting with Mr. Right isn't as hard as it seems. You can do it if you really want to. It's not always easy, but it's almost always possible. First you have to know what you want, and what's out there. Next you have to rethink or ignore the many discouraging myths that circulate about gay relationships, myths that can discourage you from looking for Mr. Right and keep you from ever finding Mr. Wonderful.

After you discount the myths meant to scare you and the silly illogical thoughts inside your head that divert you from your goals, you are ready to give some thought to your choice in a man. Some men aren't right for you. Some men aren't right for anybody, you know, those men who are never the bridesmaid, let alone never the bride. Some promiscuous men, most married men, and a few bitchy queens of infamy in gay circles are very hard to love. However, it is equally true that when you choose a man, you cannot tell right from the start who is great, who is ordinary, and who is trouble. There are plenty of rules out there for you to follow, and people even do premarital compatibility studies. But I have a better suggestion: give each reasonable possibility a chance *before* you decide to exclude him from your life.

Tactics are important too. Good tactics involve strategic planning, and giving thought and effort to realizing those plans. As with anything else, you get out of relationships pretty much what you put into them.

One strategy is always to look as good as you can. Facial features are of some importance, as is having a good body, but neither is an entirely God-given attribute. Think of how you can improve a picture by changing its frame, and work on that hair, those glasses, and that mustache and beard. Then go to the gym for a good body, and to distract yourself from those golden arch–enemies. Don't think you need great looks to be successful. If you think facial features are everything, it's because you tend to selectively notice the men who are really good-looking. Then you think you aren't good-looking on average, so what can you expect out of life, anyway. Take some time to really notice, and register, who is paired and who is single. You will find that many really handsome men are single, that many not-so-gorgeous specimens are married, and that you certainly don't have to be a poster boy to be famous with him.

Statistically, it helps to adopt a clean, neat, middle-of-the-road appearance and dress, and walk and comport yourself so that you are part of the A-Gay mainstream. Quirky and bizarre people can make it big in the gay world too, but few of us are Andy Warhol. Gay men who make their eccentricities their exclamation points, not their life sentences, do best. Gay men who have that mall quality about them wherever they are can be the ones most likely to be bought, wrapped, and eagerly taken home.

It's easiest to meet people when you have good personal qualities, and I recommended some excellent ones for you to cultivate. I do believe that nice gays finish first, because Mr. Rights lust after men with luster. The more good qualities you have and can develop, the more likely it will be that you will want what is attractive and be attractive to what you want. People only know what you tell them about yourself. If you let on that you are a winner, they probably will believe you, but if you let on that you are a loser, they will have no reason at all to doubt you.

Next comes knowing where to go to meet him, without completely wasting your time. Many gay men have their favorite cruising places and they go there and go there, though nothing ever happens. Expand your horizons and try some places you didn't think of before, or thought of before but never tried. Try the personals, try the synagogues or churches, try the Laundromat, try the Chinese restaurants at take-out time. Just don't keep trying the same impossible thing over and over again. There is a wide range of possibilities out there. Some people meet people in bars. Some people meet people in restaurants. Other people meet people in their living rooms. Of course, as I emphasize, location isn't everything, and what you do when you get there is just as important as where you go.

Now you need a few tricks for worming your way into his heart. I don't mean taking advantage of people. I do mean feeding them, and so what if a little hook is hidden in your bait. Being kind and nurturing is one of the best ways to enhance your basic allure. Another method involves pushing, but only exactly the right amount. The patients I had who stayed single when they wanted to get married were the ones who gave up too easily. The patients I had who got married when they hated being single were those who didn't say die until they were sure that a relationship was in fact terminal. Do whatever it takes to get his attention and increase the possibility that he will find you alluring and irresistible.

All these things are easier said than done if there are real obstacles on your road to success. For one thing, you may have to deal with inertia, the lure of sticking with something familiar no matter how terrible. Before you can overcome your inertia and get moving, you have to decide if you want to stay single or get married, then stick with that decision. If you want to stay single, that's OK too, as long as it's really what you want. The problem is that, at least in my experience, many gay men say they want to be single but they really don't. They want to connect, but they do nothing about connecting because they are afraid to admit that that is what they want. They don't admit it to themselves, or others, because they fear failure, fear being criticized and humiliated, or because they simply hesitate to enjoy themselves or to succeed at anything they do.

You might have to deal with being lonely. Loneliness is a very painful condition, and not everyone survives it completely intact. Some get very depressed and do self-destructive things before they have found the way out. Your main ally is recognizing that just because you are lonely now doesn't mean you will be lonely forever. In fact, painful loneliness is often a self-limiting condition—because it hurts too much for you to allow it to continue forever. Another main ally is having a good plan for overcoming loneliness. One such plan involves taking small, incremental steps without attempting to leapfrog over the problems associated with your daily situation. Solve the problem of what to do tonight, and other problems that have to be resolved right now, first, so that you can have a life, next.

There are ways to deal with rejection without avoiding dating just to avoid being rejected. Gay dating and rejection go hand in hand, so to meet someone you must be willing to experience a number of turndowns, and be able to carry on from there. There are ways to avoid being rejected too often, and ways to minimize the impact rejection has on you, but the bottom line is that the more rejections you get the better you are doing, because temporary losses mean that you are out there looking to win.

Overcoming love-aversive tendencies in yourself helps too. Gay men who recognize that they are doing things to distance themselves from possible lovers also accept that if you are having trouble finding a man and difficulty finding a committed relationship, the problem isn't only with your stars, or your genes, or with being gay in the first place—it's also with you, and what you do with what you have. Don't blame yourself, but do recognize, though that can be hard to do, that your fate is in your hands. Too often this kind of message comes across as a criticism for screwing up, but it's really a message of hope, because with a little thought and a little work, you can stop distancing and start connecting.

Low self-esteem, and the demoralization that goes with it, is one of the main reasons for keeping love at arms' length. The much over-used term "low self-esteem" really means that you don't think you have what it takes when you do, and you think you are not worthwhile enough to get what you want when you are. Many gay men have low self-esteem even though they don't act like it. They don't act like it because they cover the low self-esteem with high camp, and act like the life of a party they haven't even been invited to.

These days there is a general tendency to blame low self-esteem entirely on internalized homophobia—which is self-hatred for being gay that starts with others hating you for being queer. That's only part of the story, however. Some homophobia starts inside of you, with you alone. There is a certain unfriendliness to the instincts that isn't even a gay thing, but rather exists in everybody. As a result, you feel like a creep, hide when the welcome wagon comes by, or cannot have sex successfully because you think you are a bad missionary for doing it in the wrong position.

Gay self-hatred isn't only about one's sexuality either. Any gay man can find a whole host of reasons to dislike himself, but the result is always the same: you treat yourself shabbily, and you punish yourself, using the most efficient tool you have at hand, making it impossible for you to find Mr. Right.

It's a cliché that before anyone can love you you have to love yourself, but it's true. The cliché really means that it's hard to get people to love you if you dislike yourself, so first you need to discover why you dislike yourself, then you need to resolve to like yourself more. Liking yourself more helps you act in a way that actually enhances your self-image, both in your own eyes and in the eyes of others.

Distractions have to be overcome, too. It's so easy to get lost decorating your apartment, seeing the world, or being the life of the party. This is a time for focusing on love, not for exploring possible alternatives.

There is also reason to hope for gay men who are getting a bit older and find themselves alone. This often happens when they have broken up with a lover after some years of marriage, when a lover has died, or when they come out after years of being in—perhaps having had a wife and children in the meantime. Many either panic and act up, or go into retreat and don't act at all. There is nothing hopeless about this situation—you can still climb the mountain even when you think you are over the hill.

Sexual performance can be improved directly with hard work, devotion to the cause, and some of the gymnastics you can get out of a sex manual. However, an important basic principle is that just because you can cure impotence with Viagra doesn't mean that your impotence is caused by a Viagra deficiency. Because sex isn't confined to bed, and attitudes developed in bed spill over into your day and night life, and the other way around, fixing sexual problems often requires improving your personality and the interpersonal attitudes that are a reflection of the kind of person you are. Passivity, guilt, and impulsivity are among the many personality difficulties that negatively affect sexual performance and interfere with its maximal enjoyment, and these can be addressed.

If you aren't where you want to be after reading this book, other books, and seeing a psychotherapist, may help you. But avoid one-size-fits-all simplistic solutions to complex problems, or taking dangerous advice from friends who mainly have their own welfare at heart or want to see you fail so that they can win in the grand competition of life. Be on the lookout for helpers whose theories hold water—like a sinking boat.

Before you have the basic tools you need for seeking, finding, and keeping Mr. Right, you need to take one more step. You need to make an action-oriented plan for you from all of the possibilities outlined in this book. It's not enough to think, "Now I know what to do and how to do it." It's results that count. What good is scientifically prepared cat food that the cats won't eat? You aren't finished until you stick out your hand and someone grasps it. That is why you have to develop an action plan for life, one that starts with the desire for and ends with an actual, real-time Mr. Right. Developing an action plan means turning your approach around and doing before thinking, not the reverse. The happiest days of your life can be ahead of you if you use them well and effectively, to meet someone sweet, stable, pleasant, faithful, and loving.

Index

About the Author

Martin Kantor, M.D., is a psychiatrist who has been in full-time private practice in Boston and New York and on the staffs of The Massachusetts General Hospital and The Mount Sinai School of Medicine. He is the author of ten other books on psychological topics, including *Distancing*, which describes how people avoid relationships due to anxiety, *Homophobia*, which views homophobia as a manifestation of deep psychological problems, and *Treating Emotional Disorder in Gay Men*, which describes the form some common psychological difficulties take when they appear in homosexuals, and offers some practical suggestions on how to modify psychotherapy to make it more relevant to, and palatable and affirmative for, gay men. He lives very quietly during the week with Michael in a small house on the banks of a river in the New Jersey woods, and reverse commutes to New York City on weekends.